The Game Changer Formula

Predictable success for you, your family, and your business

Rory Prendergast

Table of Contents

Introduction 1

Part 1: Overview 7
1. Crests and Troughs 9
2. The Formula 19
3. The Impact 27
4. Your Operating System 33
5. Your Power Vision 45

Part 2: The Daily 10 65
6. The Mindset Manual 67
7. Stillness 83
8. Imagination 91
9. The Daily Review 103
10. The Daily Check-In 109
11. The Daily Planner 119
12. Movement 129
13. Hydration 137
14. Fuel 143
15. The Early 8 155

Part 3: Getting Started 165
16. Let's Get Moving 167
17. Balance 179
18. Calm Seas, Skilful Sailors 183

19. Responding to Stress 199
20. What Change Looks Like 207

Part 4: Resources 221
21. Power Vision Process 223
22. Sample Mindset Manual 253
23. Accountability Partner Scripts 259
24. Sample Meditation 263
25. Exercise Routines 267
26. Emergency Morning Routine 271
27. Recommended Books and Other Content 273
28. The Epic Project 277

Introduction

Do you feel like life could be better, that you could be more successful in work, business, relationships, or looking after yourself? Would you like to have predictable success, to have a life of significance, to make a difference or make the world a better place? Well, me too. I have struggled with success and failure and been unable to operate at a consistent level, a level that would produce predictable results.

I've had some great adventures in business and travel. I've solved impossible problems. I bounced my boat across the Atlantic and danced with diplomats in South America. Yet I have also lost a lot of money, run a businesses into the ground, and dealt with multiple personal predicaments and insecurities.

In 2008 I embarked on a huge adventure that lasted two years. I bought a boat and, with very little knowledge about how it worked, I set sail with my wife from the west coast of Ireland. We sailed down the edge of Europe, along North Africa, before turning to cross the Atlantic. Eventually we reached St. Lucia and spent the next year and a half exploring the Caribbean Islands before departing again for the return trip to Europe.

During that trip, through stormy cloud-filled days and calm and starry nights, I began the gradual work of resolving the rollercoaster highs and lows. I have now found an answer and distilled it to a simple formula. I want to share the formula that has transformed my life and the lives of other people who have applied it.

Vision, mindset, energy, and accountability are the key elements to developing predictable success. When you can implement these four elements in the right way every day, you will quickly begin to see changes in yourself, your relationships, and your work.

You may have tried planning, goal-setting, and change before. Maybe it all seemed great until it fell apart after week three. There is a simple reason that your best intentions fail more often than they succeed: Your willpower is not the best tool for change. The Game Changer Formula can bring about the change you need to develop predictable success.

If you don't take this on, here's what will happen. You will continue to live your life the same as you're doing today. Things may be okay, but you will probably not achieve your potential. You won't look back on your life with great pride, and you will have many regrets.

Imagine having complete clarity on what you need to do each day to achieve your goals. Imagine being able to change your circumstances so that what looks like a problem becomes a solution. Imagine reaching the levels you want to achieve in work, business, relationships, and your personal life.

In this book you will learn how vision, mindset, energy, and accountability are the key elements in developing predictable success.

I have worked through this process with many people, including a group of sixty people for sixty days, and when asked if it had improved their lives and their businesses, 96 per cent of respondents said that it had.

I want to teach you a simple formula and process that anyone can implement with a little commitment. If you're with me so far and are willing to take real responsibility for your own life – it's never going to be anyone else's fault anymore – then turn the page and let's get started.

But:

If you are unwilling to make some small commitments in exchange for huge return…

If you believe that other people or circumstances beyond your control are the reason for your mediocre success…

If you are unwilling to learn and keep learning…

…then STOP. Put this book away, or better still, give it to someone who is willing to take responsibility and action.

The price of greatness is responsibility. —Winston Churchill

I hope you're reading on. If you are, and if you commit to implementing the Game Changer Formula, I know that you will live a better life. You will have better relationships. You will be a better, healthier, more energetic and positive version of you. You will thrive in your business.

This will require some change. You'll need to embrace it. That's the first lesson of this book. The world is changing faster every day, and if you're not willing to embrace that, you'll be left behind.

One more thing. I am quite an impatient reader, and I like writing that gets to the point and moves on. I have tried to remove anything from this book that was not necessary to get the message across. I have looked for the simplest answers, because I believe they are more easily adopted. In refining this into its simplest form, the Game Changer Formula, I concentrate on the 20 per cent of knowledge and process that will bring you 80 per cent of the results in achieving the life you deserve.

In the chapters to come, I share excerpts from our ship's log, written in the early hours of stormy mornings and the bored, balmy days at sea. These contain the seeds of what became the Game Changer Formula, whose essence rose to the surface of my mind only because of the isolation, doubts, boredom, and battles of everyday life on the ocean. They are the strands of logic and the threads of lunacy that allowed me to get to where I am now.

> *Inaction breeds doubt and fear. Action breeds confidence and courage. If you want to conquer fear, do not sit home and think about it. Go out and get busy.* —Dale Carnegie

The book has four parts. Take them at your own pace.

Part 1: Overview

This section explains the background, the impact of the formula on different people (including myself), and why you may have failed at change before. It describes a system you can use to define your vision – in other words, how to determine your long-term goals.

Part 2: The Daily 10

This section details the process. Each step has its own chapter. The aim is to give you enough understanding to implement the process immediately. The focus is on simplicity. I could write a book on each of the ten steps, but you don't need that much detail to succeed. You need the 20 per cent of effort that will bring 80 per cent of the results, and that's exactly what you'll get.

Part 3: Getting Started

This section covers how to implement the Game Changer Formula. It identifies some challenges you may run into and shows how to deal with them. It offers further recommendations that may help you in achieving predictable success.

Part 4: Resources

This section has downloadable templates and other resources you can use. It also provides further reading materials if you want a deeper dive into any of the elements of the formula. Finally, it offers other tools and processes that I use every day to keep things on track and ensure I am continuously growing and improving.

*

In summary: There is a Game Changer Formula. You can implement it and see changes as quickly as tomorrow. To do this, I will show you a ten-step process that is easy to do. I call it the Daily 10. The next chapter explores how the process has changed my life and the lives of people with whom I have shared the Game Changer Formula.

Part 1: Overview

1. Crests and Troughs

A flying fish has just landed on my lap. It's four in the morning and I'm on the weird watch. That's the three to six AM shift. It's a solitary stretch, always. On stormy nights it's busy out here, and it has been tonight, but now I nurse a mug of tea and watch a storybook moon slip under the low hem of cloud.

We had a great run today at seven and a half knots, touching eight. We are riding a depression which should last us 48 hours and will probably kick us out into an area of high pressure, to calm water and little breeze. The seas are rough in these strong south-westerlies. We will make about 160 miles today.

Below deck we lost the cutlery drawer coming off a wave. It smashed across the galley and now lives in my bunk along with all the other homeless, damaged, and displaced items. Aside from the cutlery drawer, I now sleep with half a dozen large books, a sail, two bags of potatoes, and the toilet seat that let me down this morning. The top of the cooker, the kettle, and assorted other confused projectiles comfort Ursula in her bunk. She's asleep after a tough watch.

On deck the waves are like dogs barking over a wooden fence. The foamy snarls and white teeth indicate the desire to bite.

Experience tells you to pass the fence with confidence, but you're never quite sure if this particular dog can clear it. The odd wave does clear the sides, but when it bites it's not cold.

Tonight, as often happens on the weird watch, a stream of consciousness has opened up and I'm struggling to grasp it. I'm scratching it down in my notebook under the red glow of my head torch, because these just might be the reflections that enlighten the plot, the obscure story I have been tussling with over the past three weeks at sea. It's not quite the resolution I'm looking for, but it's getting close.

I am trying to understand why I am here, in the middle of the Atlantic Ocean, with my new wife, in charge of a yacht that I really don't know how to sail. Am I unbalanced, deranged?

The past 48 hours at sea has been quite like my 38 years on earth. There have been steep waves, high crests, and deep troughs. We've skirted a depression. There have been rough seas and calm water. I've gathered a pile of confused baggage, and I don't even know if it's mine. I've covered a lot of mileage at a good speed. We are on the crest of a wave this second, so I know what's coming next. Down I go.

It's now 12 years later. My 50th birthday is days away, and I've figured it out. I'm not unbalanced or deranged. I'm just like everyone else. I have managed to do some really interesting and fun things in my life, while some other things have not gone well at all.

I prefer highs and lows to an even keel. Moderation is never something I've been good at. —Jenny Eclair

I crossed the Atlantic Ocean on my own sailing yacht with no sailing experience. Then I did it again. I bought a hotel, operated it, and sold it for more than double my investment. I went to the Grammys and have met all kinds of people: Hollywood actors, presidents, prime ministers. I developed a $1.5 million ecommerce business from zero with my partner Kieran in just 18 months.

I co-founded and now run a franchise company. Within a year of start-up, it had franchises in all major cities across the US, Canada, Australia, New Zealand, and the UK. I have crossed paths with pirates off the coast of Africa. I speak to audiences around the world, sometimes over a thousand in size. I met my wife at a US Ambassador's party in Santiago, Chile.

While out for a run recently I saved a woman's life. I liberated a family friend from a Bangkok prison. I persuaded a bank to give me two million dollars when my only possession was a Volkswagen Golf. I closed three real estate deals, each impossible according to various lawyers, within eight hours.

I like to say that I am good at getting impossible shit done.

But I have also experienced catastrophes. Businesses that failed, relationships that I messed up, and abundant plans that never got off the ground. I drank too much, did poorly in school and college, and had times of depression and of complete confusion about what the hell I was doing. I am the guy who paid for two years of gym membership and went twice. I came within a split second of death three times – once through stupidity, once under peer pressure, and once as a result of excess alcohol.

I kept making the same mistakes over and over with money, business, relationships, and mental stability. It had become a habit. I had low self-esteem, I disengaged from normal activities, and I was often a significant pain in the ass.

It became important to me to figure out why things sometimes worked out well and I got the impossible stuff done, while on other occasions things just fell apart. Why wasn't there any consistency? These waves, crests, and troughs were too predictable.

What was going on in my life when things were going great? What was happening when they were falling apart? Answering that challenge led me to realize that some actions correlated with getting the impossible stuff done, and some appeared when life was getting on top of me and I was feeling out of control.

Putting together a list of those actions seemed the obvious thing to do. It was tough, because I was working from memories that were many years old. I read lots of books and tried to narrow down what I learned to the 20 per cent of a process that could get me 80 per cent of the results.

I had learned a lot about myself from my transatlantic sailing. Handling storms and equipment failures a thousand miles from land will do that to you. But it was only after my final conversation with my dad before he died that I realized I had to figure this stuff out.

It was obvious to my dad and me that this would be the last talk we would have. He said to me, "I could have been a better dad." We had never had a solid relationship, and I didn't know how to respond. I do now.

> Ship's Log: May 18 – Position 35:37N 36:49W – Wind SW Force 5, Speed 5.9 knots, 428 nautical miles to Horta
>
> We move 100L of diesel out of the way and lift the cockpit floor to get at the steering quadrant. Luckily what we see is repairable, and after half an hour and a refuelling for *Cerys* we are under way again on autopilot. Back to our original shifts. To celebrate I decided to go to the bathroom. As we hit an unexpected wave, I slid off and took the toilet seat with me. Another casualty for my bunk tonight. It's getting crowded in there.

I didn't want to have regrets like my dad did, so I dug deeper to figure out a way to make things work better for me and to develop the life and the predictable success that I believe we all deserve. I wish I had told my dad what I now know: that he was the best dad he could have been, and I am 100 per cent satisfied, proud of him, and lucky to have him as a dad.

It wasn't until I met a coach that I realized that my attitude and physical health played an enormous role in my successes. He encouraged me to explore how I could improve them.

Change is good… You go first.

There was another component missing. I had tried lots of methodologies for business improvement, self-development, and motivation, but I had implemented none of them consistently. I had worked on goal-setting multiple times, but if you had asked me what my goals were three weeks later, I wouldn't have been able to tell you.

When I needed help with my running, I went to an Olympic runner, Catherina McKiernan, who had a dramatic impact on my endurance and injury reduction. Now I needed help with life. I realized that I needed a coach who would work with me one to one.

When I met Jim Hickey for the first time, I unloaded all of this on him. I told him all my plans and how I wasn't concentrating on any of them. I expected us to look at goal-setting. I expected that he had a process, that he would bring me through it, and that it would focus on planning, accountability, and motivation. I waited for him to roll out the slide deck or draw the diagram, but I got none of that.

Instead, he asked me calmly and earnestly, "Will you be accountable to me?"

Jim told me that everything I needed was already within me. He pointed out the pile of clutter and negativity in my path. He explained where it came from and showed me how to get through it. It was an emotional encounter for me.

I admit I was initially sceptical of his way of working. But I trusted him and said I would give it my best shot. Something had to work; something had to change. I promised myself that day that I would do my best to follow Jim's advice for a month. If I didn't see impressive results by then, I would go back to normal, starting again with someone or something else. I promised Jim I would check in with him by text each day to let him know I was on track with my plans. That was part of the deal, part of being accountable to him. It was the start of a great relationship with Jim and the first step on a long journey of predictable success.

When I worked on transforming my mindset, the way Jim had described for me, I saw changes within 24 hours. I began by spotting small differences in my behaviour, my productivity, the way I dealt with other people, and my ability to persevere with habits that had failed me for years. It sounds bizarre, but I felt like a different person almost right away. I even paused occasionally to challenge myself: "Rory, you don't usually act like that. What's going on?"

One night, early in the process, I was travelling. I had made a commitment to run every workday, and that evening, as I pulled into the town of Fermoy just after six o'clock, I realized I had forgotten my running gear for the morning. It was on the radiator inside the front door. In small towns like Fermoy, everything closes at six, so this was a challenge.

Normal Rory would have said, "I can't run without my gear. Jim won't mind if I don't run tomorrow. I have a legitimate reason." But something had shifted. My mind wasn't operating like that anymore. I had developed into the kind of person who wouldn't let Jim or myself down by texting with that excuse.

I ran around town and knocked on every shop window until I got people's attention. That's not the kind of thing I had ever done before. Some owners or attendants opened their doors for me, as I was in such a panic, but they had shut down their point-of-sale systems for the night. No one could sell me running gear. As I trudged back to my hotel, I thought about what I had just done, and how unusual it felt.

I didn't give up. Instead of running at six in the morning, I changed my schedule so I could go into the shops when they opened at nine, and I squeezed in some time to run later in the day. Job done. I texted Jim, he was happy, and I felt a sense of power over circumstances that I hadn't experienced before.

I had found a way to frame any situation in a way that makes me feel strong, in command, and on course for predictable success.

Now, I appreciate that I am not the only person who has to deal with these trials in life, or who feels like life is getting on top of them, or who is afraid of failure in all aspects of life.

On a recent trip to the US, I met two friends I had not seen for quite a while. I had breakfast with one and lunch with the other. At breakfast my first friend told me about challenges he was having in relationships at home. I understood instantly, because they were similar to challenges I had faced myself. I knew from being open with the people close to me and with peer groups I am in that they are common issues. But my friend didn't know this, because he didn't have anyone with whom he felt he could speak candidly about these things. Once he discovered they were the same difficulties faced by many others, and that there was nothing unique about his situation, he felt relieved and empowered to find a solution.

At lunch, my second friend revealed the same concerns. Again he felt his situation was uncommon. When I told him about my previous discussion, it blew him away. He immediately relaxed, and it lifted a burden from his shoulders.

Every year, I meet a group of friends to spend 48 hours of quality time together – most of it in a pub telling old stories we all know too well already. We have developed the "bar stool of truth". It comes out late in the evening, and when you sit on it you have to tell the truth. We can ask each other any question. The questions are serious, but the same themes surface all the time: fear of failure, self-esteem, negative self-talk, and insecurities.

These are the underlying problems we need to deal with as humans. They are the concerns that guide our failures, our stress, and our lack of progression to the goals we set for ourselves.

In a study published in the *Harvard Business Review*, Vantage Hill Partners, a London-based consulting firm, surveyed 116 CEOs and other executives about their deep-seated fears. Those fears included: being incompetent, under-achieving, and appearing foolish. Five executives in their 50s (four of them millionaires, all with stable families) admitted that they feared retirement.

These fears had a serious impact on how they performed in their roles. Taking bad risks to overcompensate, being suspicious and overcautious, not speaking up, and being dishonest. This contributed to impaired decision-making and focusing on survival rather than growth.

I have learned three things from analyzing my own imperfections and seeking guidance. First, I am not alone. Second, a basic formula solves all of this. Third, you can move from survival mode to growth mode in a matter of days.

This involves change – and that's another thing most of us are frightened of. Fear of change is just fear of the unfamiliar. If you have clarity about your destination, there is no need to fear the unknown. We examine that in Chapter 18.

My good friend and mentor John Heenan is right on the money with one of his most used expressions: "Change is good… You go first."

*

In summary: I have had an interesting life, but it has had major highs and lows. I examined these to figure out if there was a formula for what enables progress and what precedes decline. With help from a coach, I discovered that most other people are in a comparable position. There is an easy path out, and you can see differences within days.

This is important because if I were to choose one factor that transformed everything for me, it would be the discovery that I already had everything I needed. It was just concealed from me, and I needed a shift in mindset to open the doors to progress. That led me to learn how my mindset was influencing me adversely, and that I could harness its power easily.

The next chapter will reveal the formula I developed for predictable success. The Game Changer Formula.

2. The Formula

This chapter provides an overview of the Game Changer Formula and the process that activates it. It also has a breakdown of the different sections in the book and how best to use it.

It may be difficult to believe, but there is a simple formula for predictable success. You can apply it to your life by changing your daily routine just a little. That small change will have a dramatic impact on your life.

> *The successful warrior is the average man, with laser-like focus.*
> —Bruce Lee

I call it the Game Changer Formula because it changes the game of life for good. You may have tried to improve the way you operate. You may have succeeded for a period, but most likely things fell apart at some point. Willpower is a crutch that is not robust enough to maintain systematic advancement.

What makes the Game Changer Formula different is that it is designed to be sustainable and continuous. It does not rely on your willpower. I developed it after years of trying to find a system that could produce the results I was looking for across all aspects of my life.

The Game Changer Formula has improved my relationships with my wife and my son. It has brought me many new and profitable business opportunities. It has increased my productivity by about 50 per cent. It has made me fitter, faster, and more flexible at 50 years of age than I have ever been before. It has had a giant impact on my self-confidence and on my attitude to the world.

It has helped me to see life as an exciting and adventurous game that can be won. So if life is a game, then this is the Game Changer Formula:

$$(\text{Mindset} + \text{Energy} + \text{Accountability})^{\text{Vision}} = \text{Predictable Success}$$

The Game Changer Formula

This book will teach you how to implement the Game Changer Formula using ten simple daily steps: the Daily 10. It will show you the course of action you can take to achieve predictable success in your life. It will explain the reasoning behind the formula and the process. Finally, it will give you the tools and resources you need to get started immediately.

This book lays out the process in a manageable, easy-to-understand system. It goes through each element to ensure you can implement everything to get to live the life you deserve. The good news is you can begin today.

If you decide to implement it fully today, you will immediately notice some subtle changes. These early changes are different for everybody, but people initially notice improvements in their productivity or mental attitude. In order for this to work, you need to do two things right now:

1. Accept that you and you alone are responsible for your own success.
2. Commit to implementing this formula for 12 days.

Take another look at the Game Changer Formula. I will now define its terms and the simple process you can use to execute it.

Vision

This is your target. It is what you want to achieve in life. It's important to know this, to ensure that your mindset and energy are moving you in the right direction. In working on what we will call your Power Vision, you will define your purpose in life and understand the different roles you play in it.

There is a process for working out your Power Vision, which is laid out in Chapter 5. You will learn how to define clear goals for your roles. Everything else you do will be directed towards achieving those goals. You'll develop a Power Vision for the life you deserve.

Mindset

In applying the process, you will place a lot of emphasis on mindset. You have a current mindset, a program on which you run your life. You will understand how your mind is wired, how your current program was created, and how it is probably interfering with the predictable success that you could achieve.

Even successful people have negative programming and self-doubt. Winners identify these doubts and reprogram them. You will learn how to use the Mindset Manual, stillness techniques, imagination, and daily reviews to edit that program. Your mindset will become your ally instead of your enemy. This may sound strange at first, but you'll soon see how it works.

Energy

Without energy, everything grinds to a halt. You will discover where to get your energy and how to maintain it, ensuring you have the fuel you need for predictable success, even as you get older.

Because you will need more power to succeed in the game of life, you will see what your body and brain need for increased performance. You will realize the impact that fuel (food), hydration, and movement (exercise) have on your performance. This will enable you to use your new mindset to achieve your potential.

Accountability

Accountability is one of the simplest things that people overlook when creating a plan for themselves. Without it, 95 per cent of us will fail to maintain the Game Changer process. You need an accountability partner to win this game. You will learn how to set that up easily.

Reading this, you may say to yourself, "That sounds like a lot of work and a lot of change." Trust me, it's not. It's just going to take a small addition to your daily routine to implement the ten-step process, the Daily 10.

Predictable success is knowing that you will achieve your aims and goals across all aspects of your life. Remember: In the past, you may have tried in vain to implement changes: giving up smoking, taking regular exercise, eating a healthier diet. You may have failed because you relied on willpower. We will look at why willpower failed you, and how you can bypass it to make life-changing adjustments quickly and easily.

This is not difficult to do. But it will require a little change and a little commitment.

Trust me: you can do this.

To get the Game Changer Formula working for you, I have broken it down to ten simple steps that you will implement daily. Each step can be as complex as you want. You could spend years studying them, trying different methods or variants, but I don't work that way. I am always looking for the 20 per cent of activity that will produce 80 per cent of the results.

That's what I have done for myself, and that's what I suggest for you. Once the process is working, you can spend all the time you want on deep dives into each step. Or you can keep it simple. I will recommend books and resources where you can gain more knowledge on each step. Feel free to dive in – but only after you have the process working for you.

You will need three things to make it work:

1. A small notebook with a hard cover – ideally something that fits in your pocket.
2. A larger notebook. I recommend A3 or a diary. Even a few sheets of paper is fine to start.
3. A commitment to yourself to take responsibility for your life and to implement the Game Changer Formula for 12 days.

You may wonder how change can happen so quickly, given that you've never been able to change before. It's because this type of change – fundamental change – is enabled by changing not the world but your perception of it. It is a game changer, and it can happen almost instantly.

The truth is, you don't see a situation the way it is. You see a version of it that is biased by your subconscious and your beliefs. Because of that, you and other people experience the same event differently. You have your own way of perceiving the world, and while it's difficult to change the world, it's easy to change your perception of it.

Your emotional state, your stress levels, and your patience can all be under your control. It may feel like your emotional state is a product of the events going on around you, but it's not. It's determined by an internal program that influences how you react. As you learn to train your subconscious mind, you will gain conscious control over your life.

Most people blame circumstances for where they are in life. They chose the circumstances that they wanted out of life, but they haven't found them yet. If you want predictable success, you need to hunt down the circumstances that are a good fit for you. If you can't find them, then you must create them.

Taking responsibility for your life, for your circumstances, and for change does not mean taking the blame for what was beyond your control. You are not to blame for the cards that have been dealt to you so far, and you should never be hard on yourself for that. But you are responsible for how you play those cards, and for finding or creating a better hand in the next round.

3. The Impact

What impact can the Game Changer Formula have on your life? In this chapter I will outline the effects it has had on my life and the lives of people I have shared it with. This will give you a sense of the benefits it can bring to you and those around you. I hope you will be inspired to follow through. You will see that this is real, it is impacting people every day, and it is generating predictable success.

> *The secret of your future is hidden in your daily routine.*
> —Mike Murdock

I never expected to be writing a book or working with people to implement the Game Changer Formula. It just happened.

As the CEO and co-founder of a franchising company, I quickly realized that what I was putting together and learning could be of huge benefit to my franchisees. The vision for our company is: "To empower and support ambitious entrepreneurs to control their own destiny by building a local business they are proud of." If I was going to empower people, what better way than to share what I had learned?

I also knew that this would benefit their businesses financially and would therefore also help our business to grow. I looked at how best to share my knowledge.

I decided to do a series of short videos every day for 60 days. It was outside my comfort zone, but I thought I should give it a shot. So I just did it. The broadcasts were simple, quick, and largely unplanned. I just spoke what was on my mind. I shot them on my iPhone as I walked or cycled to work and went through my daily routine.

The results surprised me. I've had over 30000 views of those videos – not a substantial number in YouTube terms, but at least ten times more than I had predicted. What interested me most was the survey I did at the end of the series.

First, I asked people how many days a week they were completing the morning routine – the Daily 10, as I call it now. The goal is to do it Monday to Friday, but it can take a little while to do all ten, and it's okay to take it easy. Half of the respondents were doing it five days a week, and a few people were even doing it six or seven days a week.

96% said the process made them more successful in life.

Next, I asked how they would rate the impact that the process had on them. On average, they gave it 7 out of 10. That made me happy. They gave the same rating to the routines I had outlined, making me even happier. Now I knew that what was working for me worked for other people too.

The next question aimed to determine if the process had made them more successful in their business: 80 per cent said yes.

This was a massive and unexpected result. Even better was the response rate for the last question. I asked if the process had helped them to become more successful in life in general: 96 per cent said yes. This blew my mind. I was so grateful to everybody who gave it a shot. 96 per cent!

In my own case, once I understood the process, I saw results within 24 hours – not huge changes initially, but small things. I noticed that my negativity to certain situations had disappeared. I was getting 30–40 per cent more work done in the day. I was extremely focused, and I was much more tolerant of other people. My to-do list, something I had always struggled with, was often cleared when I left my desk.

I was tired, though. The increase in exercise and the difficulty I had with sleep at the time meant I had to push through a few weeks of fatigue. We'll talk more about that later.

As my routine became more ingrained, I noticed huge differences. I wasn't tired anymore. I was fitter than I had ever been in my life. Early every morning I was running 5 kilometres (just over 3 miles) and swimming in the sea at 8 degrees Celsius (46 Fahrenheit) in the dark, and I was loving it.

In a detailed medical that I had soon afterwards, I hit all the metrics for gold standard at my age. My dietician said she rarely sees cholesterol levels like mine. That encouraged me to set a target to reach 120-plus years of age and to enjoy every minute, which has become a whole other story.

I had far more energy than I ever had before. I was able to maintain that energy and focus in late and long meetings, which had always been a challenge for me. And I achieved it without coffee, which was new. My ability to concentrate on difficult tasks was a complete game changer. It meant my productivity improved and I sometimes got to leave work early to spend more time with my wife and son.

I felt like I had changed. I felt like a new person.

With my family, I was seeing things in a new light. Situations I just wouldn't accept before, I was now open to understanding. I started looking for new ways to deal with parenting issues rather than just accepting what I thought I knew.

I was noticing new opportunities all the time, all over the place, and I developed an "I'll find a way" attitude that I applied across my business, family, and personal life. I began setting goals much higher than ever before, and I became far more confident. My self-esteem improved dramatically.

As I write this I am in Chile, and I think the process has even helped my Spanish! I haven't studied Spanish for years, but I am more confident and more open to making grammatical errors, so I try harder to get involved in conversations.

I am now consistently happier, healthier, more productive, and more successful than I have ever been in my 50 years.

I even got some of my friends engaged. One of them, Willie, recently told me he was my biggest sceptic when I first told him about it – until he tried it. Now he maintains his routine every day and holds himself accountable to me each morning.

In Chapter 20 you will find comments from people to whom I have taught the process. You may find something that will encourage and drive you to incorporate the Game Changer Formula into your day and live a significant and prosperous life.

Below, I summarize some benefits you may see. The benefits will be different for everyone, depending on the needs you have and the goals you set for yourself.

Health and fitness	Clearer direction
Better relationships	Less wasted time
Better focus	More money
Better productivity	New opportunities
Less stress	Better parenting
Business goals reached	More confidence
Better self-esteem	More energy
Better concentration	Personal goals reached
Higher goals set	More organized
To-do lists done	Better leadership

In summary: The Game Changer Formula has been implemented by people all over the world. In our survey, 96 per cent of respondents said it has made them more successful in their life. The benefits you can expect include higher income, stronger relationships, better health, and more confidence.

In the next chapter you will discover how one simple change can have a dramatic impact on your life.

4. Your Operating System

It is time to look at what drives successful change, and why people so often fail when they commit to goals despite incentives and strong motivation. The concept I'm about to explain should unquestionably be taught in schools, in my opinion, but it never is. In fact, you are probably among a tiny percentage of people who has even heard of it, never mind done anything about it.

To achieve your potential, you must understand a little about how your mind works. This chapter looks in particular at the subconscious mind: how it impacts your life, and how you can train it to help realize your ambitions.

> *These subliminal aspects of everything that happens to us may seem to play very little part in our daily lives. But they are the almost invisible roots of our conscious thoughts.* —Carl Jung

The human brain is the most complex thing in the known universe. It weighs only 3 pounds, yet it uses 20 per cent of your energy. It has a hundred billion neurons and a trillion supporting cells packed into the size of two clenched fists. Every thought you have, every emotion and experience, and every decision (an estimated 35,000 a day, 200 of them about food) is a set of communications between those neurons.

The mind is not the same as the brain. The brain is a visible, tangible organ. The mind is part of the invisible world of thought, beliefs, mindset, and imagination. The mind is mainly associated with the brain but is not confined to it. When people refer to their mind, they normally mean the conscious mind – the part that we, as humans, generally understand. It is the part of the mind that is aware, uses logic, and is responsible for voluntary actions.

Your conscious mind can't keep up with 35,000 decisions a day, because it is relatively slow and uses a lot of energy. We often become aware of a decision only after we have made it.

Your subconscious mind is already pursuing goals that you are not aware of.

Sigmund Freud was the first to map in detail the unconscious mind, the part that is hidden or below the surface. Since then, many authors have written different theories on the mind, and technology has allowed us to study activity in the brain that is associated with different parts of the mind. Many different terms are used to explain the different parts of the mind, and they can overlap: conscious mind, nonconscious, unconscious, subconscious.

When trying to decide what term to use in this book, I became frustrated. Much of what I read was contradictory. Then I returned to my 80:20 rule. Do I really care what I call it? No. Once I know how it works and can explain it so that you can also make it work, that's all that matters. I will refer to the part of the mind you need to understand as the subconscious mind. Some professionals may disagree, but that's all right with me. Okay with you?

Now I want you to use your imagination for a moment. Imagine you have anchored your yacht in the bay. You have launched your tender, a rowing boat, and you're headed to the pier, about one mile away. You've never been at this port before.

There is a channel with rocks on both sides – some are visible, and some are just under the surface. That's why the yacht wouldn't go in. You're okay, because you have a chart and you have planned your approach to the pier. This will be easy.

For some reason, though, when you point your boat towards the pier, it drifts towards the rocks. You adjust your course and keep rowing, but it drifts back. Again and again you adjust course, but you keep drifting towards those rocks. You're getting tired. Your energy is going, and you begin to feel that this will end badly.

You felt you were in control. You row every day; you're strong and fit. The boat is well built and adequate for the job. The weather is good and there is no wind; the bay is calm. This should be easy. But you can't reach your destination. You keep drifting into the rocks. What the hell could be wrong?

You decide that if things keep going like this, you won't have enough energy to reach the pier – you'll hit the rocks and sink.

Something has to change, so you stop and rest. You take ten deep breaths. You calm your mind and think. What could it be?

Then you realize. There is a current, a very strong current, pushing you towards the rocks. You can't see it, but it's there. This current is far bigger than your boat, far stronger than you, and it flows against your intended course. It's invisible – you never knew it was there, and you're not the first person to get into trouble on this stretch of water.

Now that you know there's a current, you have options. There is time to consider your response.

Will you let the current push you onto the rocks and sink your boat?

Will you persevere and maybe summon a last reserve of energy to row to shore?

Or will you just row across the current for five minutes to a point where you can go with the flow? There is a point where the current will carry you and your boat towards the pier swiftly and easily. All you have to do is use the oars for a little steerage and docking.

Suddenly your day has gone from panic about sinking and drowning to a calm and effortless row to shore. It's even enjoyable.

Do you ever find yourself pushed onto the rocks in life?

It happens. You have a plan and a clear goal, but for some reason you hit the rocks. Have you noticed it's the same kinds of rocks you run into all the time? That's because that current really exists.

It's your subconscious, and it could be pushing you onto the rocks right now, making it more difficult for you to reach your goals.

How long do you think you can row against that current?

Another way of looking at the subconscious is as your operating system. That's the software that runs a computer, managing its memory and processes. Your operating system is your subconscious mind. Your conscious mind is the apps you have installed, like Word or Excel.

The conscious mind is relatively slow. It can handle 2,000 bits of information a second and uses a lot of energy to keep impulses running at 150 miles an hour. It holds one thought at a time. The subconscious mind can handle four hundred billion bits of information a second, with impulses travelling at 100,000 miles an hour. (Studies vary on the speeds, but the bottom line is that it's a lot more powerful, and it can multitask.)

Think about the last time you drove on a busy highway. You're travelling about 80 miles an hour in busy traffic, watching your speed, navigating, judging distances, watching cars and trucks in front and behind, merging, changing speed. You're seconds away from one distracted driver causing a major accident and possibly death. And you're bored – so you pull out your phone!

How can that happen? How can you handle all that data and not even remember the last five miles? How can you have all that going on and still get bored enough to pick up your phone? It's because your conscious mind chose the destination but your subconscious mind drove you there.

MOST OF THE MIND IS BELOW THE SURFACE

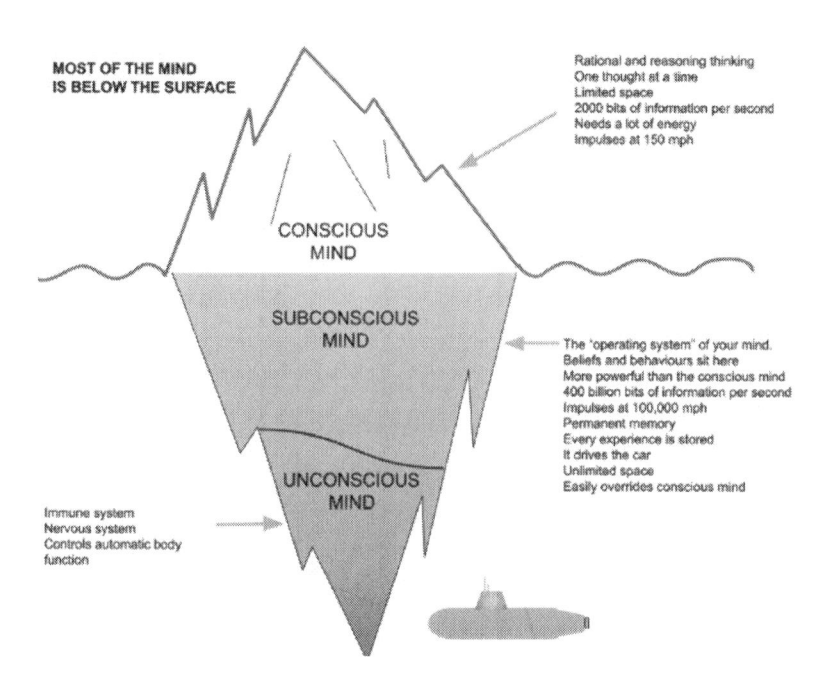

Conscious Mind:
Rational and reasoning thinking
One thought at a time
Limited space
2000 bits of information per second
Needs a lot of energy
Impulses at 150 mph

Subconscious Mind:
The "operating system" of your mind.
Beliefs and behaviours sit here
More powerful than the conscious mind
400 billion bits of information per second
Impulses at 100,000 mph
Permanent memory
Every experience is stored
It drives the car
Unlimited space
Easily overrides conscious mind

Unconscious Mind:
Immune system
Nervous system
Controls automatic body function

Your subconscious is an operating system that has been programmed since you were born. We all have one. We've programmed ourselves and been programmed by events and experiences in our past. Part of that program works with us, but much of it works against us.

Your subconscious remembers everything you have gone through since you were a child, and it uses that to build a belief system. The criticisms, the failures, and anything else negative that's happened to you will program your subconscious. You can accumulate quite a bit of negative programming from childhood, as you can imagine. That programming creates your beliefs.

In a 2015 study on the ratio of praise to criticism used by parents, most reported praising their children often and criticizing them rarely. In practice, however, parents were observed to criticize their children nearly three times as often as they praised them. That criticism is stored in the subconscious as negative programming. The beliefs you develop from it become the windows through which you view the world.

A survey in the UK found that by the age of fourteen, 98 per cent of children have a negative self-image and feel insecure. It's no wonder you're not living the life you deserve – you don't have the time or energy, because you're so busy trying to overcome this negative self-image. (It's worth noting that the word *personality* comes from the Latin *persona*, which was a mask worn by actors.)

Throughout your life the experiences you have had, both good and bad, have programmed your subconscious mind, and that is what dictates who you are, how you think, when you give up on something, where you are going, and what biases you have, good or bad.

Your subconscious mind is already pursuing goals that you are not aware of. This might sound great at first, but what if those goals are based on negative beliefs from past experiences that don't serve you well? That would be counterproductive.

Now think about this. If you know you have an operating system that acts like a current and often drags you into the rocks, don't you think you should do something about it?

Well, that's what you will do. You will rebuild that operating system so it works *for* you, twenty-four seven. You will align it with your goals so that the current carries you towards your chosen destination.

The great news is that it's easy to do this. And once it's done, your life will be changed forever. You will see things differently, you will spot new opportunities, you will be more aware of how you react to situations, and you will build better relationships. Whatever it is you decide you want out of life, rebuilding your subconscious operating system will have a massive impact on getting you there.

One of the reasons you fail so often in life – whether it's an exercise routine, a diet, a business, or a relationship – is that your willpower is weaker than your subconscious mind. You think your conscious mind is in control. It's not. Your subconscious mind is doing most of the work – because it can, and because it uses less energy to complete the task. It is also much more powerful and can process far more than your conscious mind.

The key programs of human behaviour are not logic and willpower, as you may have assumed. They are habit and imagination. These will be addressed in the Daily 10.

I discussed my theory recently with a psychologist, who explained to me that willpower alone is not enough for us to make substantial change. Willpower ebbs and flows throughout the day, the week, and the month. It's low when you are tired, hungry, or out of sorts. Even scarcity of money or time can affect your decision-making if you are just relying on willpower.

Think of change as trying to hold down a spring with your willpower. The spring is your subconscious, and it always wants to go back to its original position. As soon as you get hungry or tired, your willpower weakens and the spring pops back up.

It's like rowing against the current – it's possible to make it with immense, sustained effort if you are a long-distance rower, but if you're an ordinary person like me you need all the help you can get. You want to enjoy life, not spend it rowing against the current. You need to do things differently.

So you see it's not enough to be inspired, to be motivated, or to think happy thoughts. It's not enough to say you're going to eat less so you can lose that belly. The trick is not to commit your conscious mind to change but to commit your *subconscious* mind. As a human being, you can only handle so much discrepancy between your subconscious beliefs and your conscious thoughts and actions.

To keep a habit going, willpower must be supported by volition or structure. You need a structure to help you get out there on the bad days, a plan for what you'll do when you forget the running shoes or when there's no gluten-free option on the menu. That structure is your subconscious mind.

This book will show you how to build structure by training the subconscious mind. That way you won't need to depend solely on willpower. You will work with your subconscious, supported by your structure, and that's how you will achieve success in life.

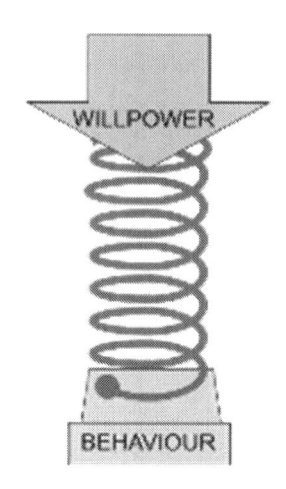

The good news is that it's easy. You just need to do two things to change it all:

1. Commit the subconscious mind to change.
2. Create a structure to maintain that change.

To make these changes, you will use elements of the Daily 10 in Part 2 of this book.

*

In summary: The subconscious mind is your operating system. Its job is to ensure you operate in a way that is consistent with your current internal program. That system has been built over years with the experiences you've had since childhood.

The subconscious mind can sometimes help you, but it is often a hindrance. If you are intent on having the life you deserve and achieving your potential as a human being, then you'll need to rebuild your subconscious and maintain its new structure.

You probably have some habits, ideas, or attitudes that you don't like but that won't go away. They are examples of the subconscious mind driving your thoughts without your conscious mind even being aware of it. Your subconscious wants to keep you on the track it has become used to, repeating the same old story, driving you towards the rocks.

In the next chapter you will learn how to uncover what you really want out of life, so you can direct your new operating system in the right direction for you. I will describe and explain how to develop a Power Vision, a focus, and a direction for all your activity.

5. Your Power Vision

Do you ever get the feeling that there's a better way to live? Do you find that you have less and less free time? That even though you're working hard, you are not making progress to where you need to be?

One possible factor is that you don't really know where you want to go. You may have done some planning, you may even have implemented that plan for a while, but you wouldn't be reading this if everything was going according to that plan.

In this chapter you will learn how to build a Power Vision to guide you to predictable success.

> *Our goals can only be reached through the vehicle of a plan, in which we must fervently believe, and upon which we must vigorously act. There is no other route to success.* —Pablo Picasso

I fell into a life that I didn't plan. I was in the hotel business because it ran in my family. My grandfather, my parents, and three of my siblings were in the hotel trade. I had chosen that path, but without clarity or a vision. It was a mistake. If you don't have a plan for yourself, you will end up part of someone else's.

To live the life you deserve, you need a clear vision of what that looks like. It's not a simple task, but if you do this, it may be the most significant thing you will ever do.

In the Game Changer Formula, you will see that mindset, energy, and accountability are all "to the power of" vision. This is important. If you don't have the right vision for you, everything will go in the wrong direction, and you will not achieve predictable success. That's one of the reasons I call it the "Power Vision".

There was one period in my life when I learned more than I had ever learned before: between 1 May and 21 December 2008. My wife, Ursula, and I untied our new 42-foot Beneteau sailing yacht, *Cerys*, from the pier at Roundstone, a fishing village on the west coast of Ireland. The yacht would be our home for the next two years. We knew little about sailing or how the boat worked, but we had absolute clarity on our vision: to get *Cerys* and crew safely to St. Lucia before Christmas.

We were not sure how we would do it. We didn't even know what impact it might have on a couple that had been married just six months. Living in such a small, isolated space could be challenging, and sometimes we spent weeks at sea without seeing another person apart from Ursula and the crew: Jeannot and Tom on the outward leg and Joey, Flanno and Tom on the return. But we knew the destination, we knew the timeframe, and we had a pretty good idea of what we didn't know. Everything else could be figured out if we took it step by step.

The Power Vision is more about who you will become than what you want to achieve. It is a subtle but profound difference.

Almost eight months after leaving home, we made it to St. Lucia. We were still married, still speaking to each other, and still alive. We could never have made that trip without a vision. A vision is a picture of your future based on your defined values. It forms the foundation for all your plans and interim goals. It is the longest-term view you will take.

Our vision was crystal clear for that voyage. At the time, I was only beginning to understand the power of having a vision. I didn't have one for my life or our lives, but we both had one for that voyage. We had to. We needed a common vision so we could get through the thousands of challenges we would encounter in those eight months. When you have a vision, you don't need to know all the steps from A to Z – you only need to know the next few.

This was the process we used to define our vision.

Uncover what we wanted

I wanted a huge adventure – something to do with the sea, and something I could not do with my current skill set.

In 1976, aged six, I watched the *St. Brendan*, a boat made of animal hides sewn together, sail off from Brandon Creek on the south coast of Ireland. The voyage was undertaken by Tim Severin to prove that the legend of St. Brendan was possible. St. Brendan the Navigator was an Irish saint who is said to have discovered America in the sixth century. Christopher Columbus referenced texts on this voyage to support his theory that lands lay on the other side of the Atlantic.

I met Tim Severin on the day he set off, as my dad had been involved in the margins of the project. I believe that experience affected my subconscious and eventually brought me to sea in 2008.

> Ship's Log: October 8 – Position 42:07.347N 008:50.735W – Wind SW Force 2
>
> Bayona: Landfall of the *Pinta* on Columbus's return from the New World was March 1st, 1493. This was the first town to hear news of the discovery. That is of course with the exception of Ardfert almost 1,000 years earlier (St Brendan The Navigator). The *Pinta* is a caravel type vessel, its real name unknown. *Pinta*, meaning painted, was a nickname. Of course it was made of wood, as Columbus was a vegan and refused to sail in a leather vessel. I had always assumed that Columbus had been at sea for years, but he only left in August 1492. He must have wanted to be back by St Patrick's Day. In fact the *Pinta* (a replica of which is moored here) was able to do up to 15 knots and frequently had to wait for the *Nina* and the *Santa Maria*. She was 20m and 7m beam with a crew of 26 and weighed 60 tons.

Decide on a destination and date

Ursula and I decided to join a rally from the Canary Islands to St. Lucia, as it appeared the safest way for us to achieve our goal. Little did we know that after the first night at sea, we would hardly see another boat for three weeks. Not as safe as we thought.

The Atlantic Rally for Cruisers (ARC) became our focus, and apart from our own safety it was all we thought about. Every decision we made had to fit this focal point. So our vision for the trip was to get *Cerys* and crew safely to St. Lucia before Christmas.

Determine the crew roles

We needed to figure out what roles had to be filled to achieve the goal. Ursula could concentrate on certain skills, and I could study others. We didn't have time for both of us to learn everything. For example, I had to understand how to fix engines, while she learned celestial navigation. Before this I could barely change a wheel.

I include new equipment here as well as skills. We learned about the boat and the challenges we would face in the mid-Atlantic: everything from handling storms to generating electrical power and ensuring we had enough water. We figured out what new equipment we needed to acquire and install for the trip. Again, it was all step by step.

We also had to determine if we needed other crew members. After our first full week at sea, it became apparent that we would need help on longer passages, as we were exhausted sailing 24 hours a day.

At every port, we made modifications to the boat, adding equipment or upgrading what we had. We read continuously and spoke with other sailors to soak up as much information as we could. We took courses on subjects like survival at sea, engine maintenance, and navigation.

Plot the course

We needed to obtain charts of all the areas we would sail through, to plot our intended course. This meant identifying obstacles, dangers, strong currents, shipping lanes, and difficult harbours. We chose the safest course possible. Even with all the electronics currently available, we plotted the course on paper charts first. If we were hit by lightning and all the electronics were fried, we would need those paper charts – and Ursula's celestial-navigation skills – to find our way home.

We also needed to plot the dates and times of the rally start and check-in times. We had to estimate how long the voyage would take us so that we could plan for food, water, and fuel.

Sail 100 miles a day

Finally we were at sea, as well organized as we could be, given our newly gained skills and tight timeframe. We were venturing into the unknown, nervous but not afraid. We had a destination, clear roles, rules for working together on board, and the right equipment to the best of our knowledge and budget. The course was plotted, and, for now at least, there was nothing more we could do in those areas. Going to sea gave me a sense of relief, because what was onboard was onboard. That was all we had. There were fewer decisions to be made.

We needed to point the boat at St. Lucia and keep her pointed there 24 hours a day, seven days a week, while we dealt with all the things that could put us off course. Many challenges arose: storms, equipment failures, personal failures, fatigue, seasickness, pirates, and the odd flying fish that would hit you in the face in the dark at three in the morning.

> Ship's Log: May 17 – Position 34:50N 39:40W – Wind SW Force 6–7, Speed 7.7 knots, 576 nautical miles to Horta
>
> 22:00, going back on watch, all Velcroed up in heaviest weather gear, only hands and eyes protruding. We mistake each other in this gear. Raising my head over the companion way, I see that Joey has taken, and dealt with, the worst of it. I left him two hours ago in 5–6 metre steep seas, force 7, *Cerys* sliding sideways off waves. Under three reefs we were running at 7.7 knots. Now, under a starry and lunar sky, seas are down to 1 metre and we are doing 6 knots. I feel overdressed. The only sea I'm getting is a docile ocean spray as two occasional waves collide to windward. I am sure somebody somewhere is paying $150 in a day spa for similar treatment.

We broke the voyage down to 24-hour slots, and our goal was to cover 100 nautical miles in each. We often had to adjust the plan because of the challenges named above.

As it turns out, *Cerys* was never actually pointed at St. Lucia – she was always off course, thanks to heavy seas, adverse wind, and sailboat design. So we spent our days and nights focused on the destination and continuously adjusting course to be as close as possible to the target. Sometimes we were pointing at the Falkland Islands, sometimes New York; hardly ever the right bearing for more than ten seconds.

But we had our vision, we knew our destination, and we had a timeframe. And all those thousands of adjustments got us into Rodney Bay, St. Lucia, in the early hours of 21 December.

I follow a similar process now for determining my vision and planning. I form a clear picture of what I want from my life, based on my values. Every decision I make has to fit into that vision. If it doesn't, then it's bringing me in the wrong direction.

Remember when we talked about power? All these micro-decisions, actions, attitudes, improvements, and adjustments, combined, are the power that drives a vision to become a reality. It's the equivalent of my 100 nautical miles a day towards my destination – being consistent every day, and adjusting every day. I engage that power and try to improve it by 1 per cent a day, creating a compound effect that accelerates me towards that vision.

How do I do this? By creating the right mindset, ensuring I have enough energy, and measuring every day through accountability. The Daily 10 process that we will discuss later becomes your power, your traction.

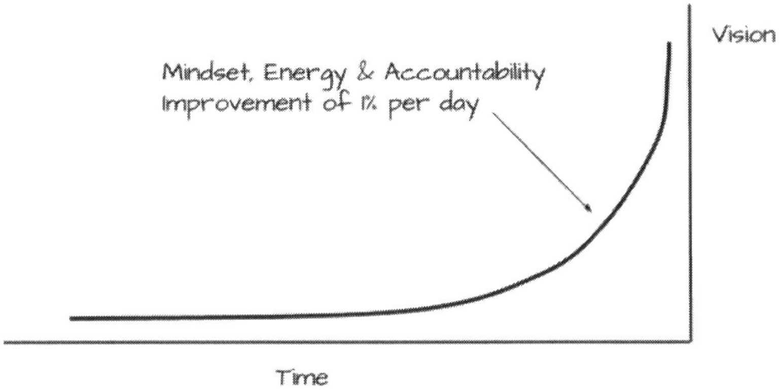
Vision
Mindset, Energy & Accountability
Improvement of 1% per day
Time

My vision and planning process today works like this (see Power Vision Workbook, Chapter 21):

1. Discover what you want
2. Create your Power Vision
3. Determine your roles
4. Develop your plan
5. Implement through the Daily 10

Discover what you want

Who are you now, and who do you want, or deserve, to be?

I have learned since the Atlantic trip that a powerful vision, which I call a Power Vision, is more about who you will become than what you want to achieve. It is a subtle but profound difference. You have complete control over who you become.

In this first step, you will determine your passions, skills, and current resources. Discovering what you want to become involves a lot more reflection than most people expect, but there are hints in your best achievements and your proudest moments. This part of the process will identify those hints and your strengths and weaknesses.

Create your Power Vision

Using what you discovered in the previous step, you will create a vision for yourself that will become your focus. Like our sailing destination of St. Lucia, that vision will guide everything. Every time you make a decision, you will ask, "Is this getting me closer to [my vision] or further away from it?"

Determine your roles

You play different roles in life. Some are more important at different times than others. Understanding that you have different roles will reduce conflict between the goals that you set for different areas of your life. This will reduce stress. It will also allow you to put targets in place for each role and to ensure that each gets adequate attention.

For example, there is little point being successful in business if your family is falling apart because of your lack of consideration for that role. People often forget that.

Develop your plan

This is plotting the course for your life. Just like in the boat, you can determine many of the challenges you may face, but you cannot know everything. That's why your plan should be divided into a three- to five-year plan, 12-month and quarterly plans, and shorter-term plans. You'll also have a daily plan as part of the ten-step process.

Each of these planning levels informs the others. The three- to five-year plan will be broad, the 12-month and quarterly plans will have some detail, and the daily plan will include everything for the day. The plan will be concise and easy to change. Remember, change is inevitable – embrace it and thrive on it.

Implement through the Daily 10

Your vision and three- to five-year plan will trickle down to your 12-month plan, which trickles down to your quarterly plan and finally to today's plan. Because of this trickle-down effect, you only need to focus on today's plan, because it fits into the quarterly plan and from there to the vision. To achieve your vision, you will use the ten-step process, the Daily 10, every day. That's covered in Part 2 of the book.

I am involved in a business owners group called Power Seven, founded and run by my friend and mentor Barry Walsh. There are seven of us in the group. A few years ago we spent two full days together to get clarity on our visions. I have used the framework from that session to create a workbook in Chapter 21, which will walk you through:

- determining what you want
- creating your Power Vision
- developing your plan
- engaging the power via the Daily 10.

If you want to be successful in life, you need a Power Vision that is true to you. When you start work on this, I encourage you to have fun – but don't take it too lightly. Don't force it if it doesn't come. You can always try again, and sometimes you just need to let go and it will come to you. You may not have two days this week to plan the rest of your life, but you can do it step by step over time.

I recommend that you incorporate the following when you work on your vision:

- light exercise
- meditation
- calmness
- nature
- fun.

Try to do it somewhere you won't be distracted and are unlikely to bump into friends – ideally outside, but that may not be possible. A hotel or library are also good places to go. When I did it with Barry and our group, we rented cabins in the woods, and I believe that guided the outcome.

Even if all you can do right now is go for a walk – take it. If there's no plan, there's no outcome, and no predictable success. When you get it right, you will spot opportunities that fit your vision. Your decision-making will become easier. You will notice opportunities arrive like waves that lift your boat, pushing it forward. Your vision will help you choose the right waves to ride.

In an ideal world, you could take two days off and start on this tomorrow. You could then build out the rest of the formula and get everything working within a few days. If you can do that, great, but for most people that won't be an option.

I strongly believe that even if you cannot take time to work out your Power Vision, you should still continue the process. Begin implementing the rest of the formula, including the Daily 10, because the longer you leave it, the less likely you are to engage with it.

That may sound contradictory. How can you implement the rest of the formula without the vision? But here's one thing I have learned. If you wait a few weeks, it will slip away. Trust me on this – I know a little about forming habits and routines that can change your life.

I urge you to start by building the Daily 10 habit. You will see benefits even without the Power Vision – and you can add that later. I'll even bet that implementing the routine will give you a far better chance of getting around to creating your Power Vision and doing it right.

A few other things to note when doing this.

If you have written your goals, then you are in the 3 per cent of people in the world to have done so. People who do not set serious goals tend to aim low. If you aim low, then that is what you will achieve.

People tell themselves they cannot do certain things or attain certain levels because of age. Age is largely in the mind – there's no reason you can't keep achieving high standards as you get older, so eliminate that thought when creating your vision.

You may be afraid to trust yourself. Pay no attention to weaknesses, lack of knowledge, or personal fears. These can all be overcome. Jump right in with both feet.

It's difficult to set clear goals initially, but once you do it and implement the Game Changer Formula, you will achieve them almost effortlessly. In fact, being unreasonable with your goals is not unreasonable. Just make them pragmatic. Who is to say you cannot achieve them?

I had a meeting once with a business partner in one of our ecommerce companies. We were ecstatic at the daily sales over a six-week period, and it looked like we could maintain that level, which would mean we had an extremely healthy business. I told my partner at the end of the meeting that we could double that daily revenue. It sounded crazy, but he was open to it, so we devised an online ad strategy and worked late into the night to implement it. We doubled our revenue 24 hours later. That is the power of being unreasonable.

At a meeting this year, the same partner suggested we aim for ten times the previous year's revenue. I immediately agreed, and we are putting plans in place to achieve that goal. We took on another partner and are on the march to ten times revenue. We may fail at some challenges along the way – something like this is never plain sailing. Failure is an occasional frustration on the path to predictable success. What if we only get halfway? Well, that's a lot better than if we had made a plan to grow revenue by 20 per cent.

Keep your vision, values, and objectives in the positive. No negative words. When I wanted to do my first triathlon, one of the best pieces of advice I got was to always look at where you want to go, not at what you might crash into. You'll end up where you are looking. Racing drivers use the same concept. Too often we fixate on where we don't want to go, then we wonder how we ended up just there.

Your subconscious doesn't understand the negative. If it hears "rock", then that's where you're headed. Ask someone not to think of a green horse, and that's precisely what they will think of. So for example, don't write, "I don't want to have any money problems next year." Use the positive: "Next year I will make 200,000 dollars."

Decision-making is easy when you have a clear vision. Just run everything by that vision, and you'll intuitively know the answer.

We were sailing from the Canary Islands to the Caribbean. On a sailing yacht, the shortest distance between two points is not necessarily a straight line. We were trying to catch the trade winds that blow west, north of the equator, and there wasn't much wind to be found. We kept heading south, hoping to find a useful breeze to get us on our westerly course, and we found ourselves off the coast of Africa.

> Ship's Log: Nov. 30 – Position 18:38.275N 026:41.718W
>
> We have been hunting for the trade winds and thought a few times we had found them. Now, just under 19 degrees north, I think we are there. We have gybed and turned west on a course of 260 directly towards St. Lucia. At last the butter has melted.
>
> Tonight the wind is sweet and very warm, all 25 knots of it. Gusting up to 29. We have taken two reefs in the main and rolled in a quarter of the genoa [a large triangular headsail]. The sliver of evening moon has set and we bumble along in the darkness.

I was on a night shift, and I got to my bunk pretty late. When I awoke, around four in the morning, there was some commotion among the crew. They were concerned about a boat that our radar said was on a collision course with us. Normally that's not a big deal, because there's plenty of space to manoeuvre. But as we got closer, my crew realized there was something odd about it. They thought someone may be in trouble. The boat was not moving as it should and was showing incorrect navigation lights.

As it approached, we tried to make radio contact. When the crew explained the situation to me, it was clear there was a possibility that someone was in trouble and that we could help. But I could also see risk. Those waters are well known for piracy, and we were an easy target. I reviewed our vision: Get *Cerys* and crew safely to St. Lucia before Christmas. Every word in our vision has a meaning. Get *Cerys* and crew *safely*… My decision was an easy one.

There was a chance that someone on the other boat wanted to do us harm. We switched off all lights and automatic radar reflectors, turned on our engine, and set a course back out to sea as quickly as we could. We kept motoring until we had put 30 nautical miles between *Cerys* and the other vessel. Obviously if we had been sure someone was in trouble, we would have helped. But clarity on our vision made evasion the only viable decision.

My lawyer tells me he finds it difficult to understand how I make decisions so quickly. To me it's simple. I know where I am going, so whatever gets me there quickest is the best call.

My Power Vision is: "Liberating ventures and family adventures". It took me a long time to get it this short, but I can break it down and talk to you about it for three hours. In the next part of the book, I will show you how my Daily 10 is the power that drives me towards my Power Vision. But first here's one important thing.

Your Power Vision is a long-term goal. If you are focused and follow the Game Changer Formula, you will get there – but you need to be happy each step of the way. People with a long-term goal achieve results faster than they expect. You will overestimate what can be done in one year and underestimate what can be done in five or ten years.

But you will not have a great life if you are always living for next week. You need to know the plan, and you need to understand the next steps, but you must live in the present and be happy with where you are.

Liberating ventures and family adventures, for me, breaks down into five Fs which are the important things in my life – what I value most:

- Family and friends
- Force 8 (my adventure "F")
- Framework
- Freedom
- Fitness.

I don't expect this will make sense to you, but each element has a story to it and reflects my values and my family's values. It also reflects the values of business partners I have chosen to work with and of friends that I respect.

Let me leave you with this question: If you carry on as you are, will you achieve your goals? The answer is almost always no, yet people still carry on the way they are. Don't be one of those people.

*

In summary: The elements in the Game Changer Formula – mindset, energy, and accountability – are "to the power of" vision. Vision carries you in the right direction: it is where you apply power. Your Power Vision is determined first by understanding your values and creating a picture of the future that fulfils those values and your desires. It is important to get your vision right, or you will apply power in the wrong direction and never achieve predictable success.

The good news is that there is a process to help you define your vision. It can take time to get it right, but don't let that stop you implementing the Game Changer Formula. Start first, then circle back to the vision once you see some progress.

The next part of the book will describe each step in the Daily 10 and how you can use them to achieve predictable success.

Part 2: The Daily 10

6. The Mindset Manual

In this chapter, you will learn how to use a tool called the Mindset Manual to develop your mindset and produce a sense of flow and ease as you move towards your Power Vision.

> *If you think you can do a thing or think you can't do a thing, you're right.* —Henry Ford

If your mindset is firm and inflexible, life will be difficult. I should know – I was like that for years. I thought it was a way to show strength of character and clarity of direction. But it led to a lot of conflict with people I was close to. Adopting a more flexible, growth-oriented mindset opened many doors for me and deepened my relationships. A flexible mindset is your friend.

Mindset is the first component of the Game Changer Formula, and for good reason. It is the element you need to set up to leverage the power of the subconscious mind (Chapter 4). Aligning your mindset with your ambitions will empower you to focus on appropriate activities, generate energy, and commit to accountability. This will lead you to predictable success.

> Ship's Log: May 12 – Position 32:22N 52:15W – Wind N Force 4, Speed 5 knots, 1,213 nautical miles to Horta

Foul-weather gear donned at dusk. We had been expecting a wind shift from SW to N, but we didn't expect it to happen in under 3 seconds. A squall appeared out of nowhere. The sea turned from blue to dark grey, and the wind speed shot up from 15 to 38 knots. It possibly went higher, but we didn't have time to look. We were under full sail, and as *Cerys* heeled violently we steered to leeward to take the pressure off, only to find another 180 degree shift. It caught us unaware and put us under pressure for about ten minutes. We got our reefs in and got quite wet in the process.

This is now ordinary. It's life on board. It's our lives. We have made a complete shift of mindset, all of us.

What is your mindset?

We need to define mindset for the Game Changer Formula. Your mindset is the set of beliefs that constitutes your approach, your responses, and your interpretations of events, resulting in a movement towards or away from a vision or goal.

Mindset straddles the conscious and subconscious, helping ideas to flow between them. You learned in Chapter 4 that the conscious mind can train the subconscious, and the subconscious mind influences conscious actions and ideas. So by focusing on mindset, you will gain the ability to influence both conscious and subconscious thoughts and actions. When this happens, you can focus them on your vision. Then you are on the path to predictable success.

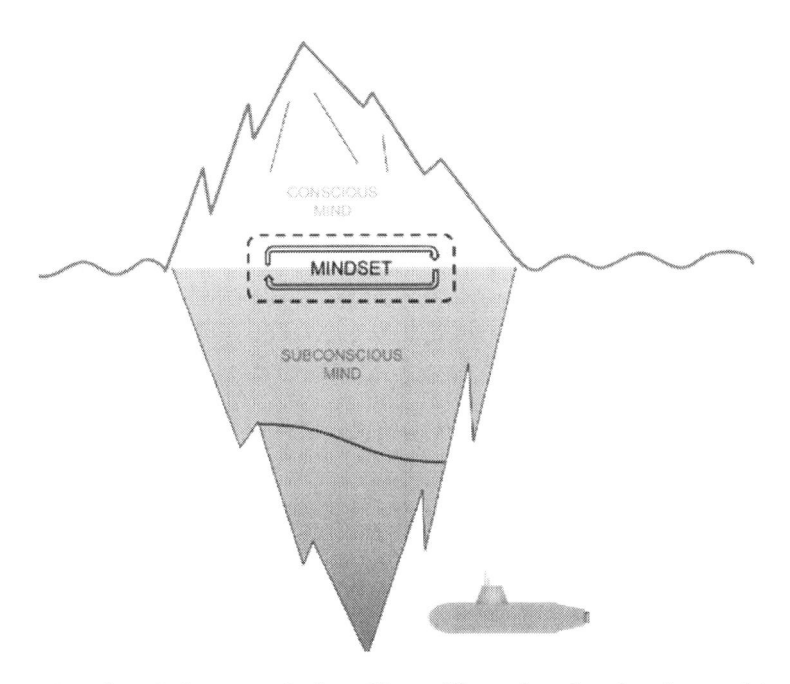

You already have a mindset. You will need to develop it to achieve the life you deserve. Your new mindset will be the result of training, using three tools from the Daily 10:

1. Mindset Manual
2. Stillness
3. Imagination.

This chapter focuses on the first tool. The second and third tools will be covered in the chapters that follow.

What is the Mindset Manual?

The Mindset Manual is like the owner's manual for your mindset. You will write it yourself, in the form of statements or affirmations composed in a specific format that will help transform your current mindset into one that cultivates predictable success.

You will now learn how to build your Mindset Manual. When Jim, my coach, first told me about this, I was sceptical but promised to give it a shot. After seeing modest but very positive results within two days, I was convinced that it was an effective tool for transformation.

I ask you now to make the same promise. It may take longer than two days for you to see positive results, but please just step outside your comfort zone for a few minutes a day over the next ten days, and you will understand what I mean.

If you are still unconvinced, or afraid of what people will think, just do it anyway and don't tell anyone. Nobody needs to know. They may notice a difference in you over time, and they may ask. But by then you will be well able to handle it.

Don't worry if you haven't got your Power Vision Workbook completed yet. You can build a basic Mindset Manual straight away, which will become even more powerful when you add the vision components.

How to start your Mindset Manual

There are three steps to getting the Mindset Manual working for you:

1. Buy a simple pocket-size blank notebook, ideally with a hard cover.
2. Build your pilot manual using the blueprint on the following pages.

3. Spend ten minutes reading the Mindset Manual first thing each morning.

(when you get your notebook send me a photo via my social channels or by email and I will give you a shout-out all contact details at www.roryprendergast.com)

What you put into your manual are straightforward affirmations that are personal to you. To affirm is to proclaim a strong positive belief in or commitment to a concept. So an affirmation is a statement of intent, resolve, and promise.

Your subconscious mind cannot differentiate between reality and imagination, fact and fiction. This is why dreams feel real. So if you create affirmations in a specific configuration, you train your subconscious to believe them. These subconscious beliefs become the roots of your conscious thoughts. That is what will change your mindset and empower you to achieve anything you want, without relying on weak willpower.

It's not about changing your habits but how you see yourself as a person. You change what you believe, at the deepest level possible. You change the way you perceive the world. When you do that, change is unforced and calm. You can transform the way you live and can achieve the life you deserve with little effort.

This is a game changer.

It's important to remember that the manual alone will not get you to your desired destination. You need mindset, vision, energy, and accountability. If you remove any of these components from the formula, it no longer equals predictable success.

I will show you two versions of the Mindset Manual, the pilot version and the complete version. Use the pilot until you have completed the vision workbook, then you can add its vision elements and build the real power of direction into the Game Changer Formula. So the pilot version becomes the complete version.

The pilot version will get you started, allowing you to see some positive results quickly. That will provide the encouragement to create your Power Vision and move to the next step. If you have already developed your Power Vision, you can go straight to the complete version of the manual.

The pilot will have affirmations applicable to most people, in my experience. Leave out one or two if they don't fit you, and add a couple that you feel will serve you, using the phrasing suggested below.

Remember the three steps for your Mindset Manual: buy a notebook, build the manual, then read the manual daily. Here's how to go about those steps.

1. **Buy a notebook** (don't forget to send me the photo)

Get a pocket notebook. Do not do this on your phone, laptop, or other digital device. Trust me on this – it is far more likely to fail you. I use a hardcover notebook about six inches by four, with a ribbon bookmark and an elastic to keep it closed. You will write in this notebook in large, easy-to-read letters. Each page will have a single affirmation; the opposite page will remain blank (see image below).

Why is it that I love ....

1. **Build your manual**

Leave some space for the complete version of the manual – you can easily rewrite, add to, or modify the manual at any stage.

Most of the affirmations start with *"Why is it that I love…"*. This phrasing can sound sentimental to some readers, and it seemed odd to me at first, until Jim explained it to me. There are four elements to it: (a) emotion, (b) positive perspective, (c) question, and (d) present tense.

(a) Emotion

Your mind has too many thoughts, and you don't have time to consider most of them. So it is difficult to remember or engrain any of them as ideas or beliefs. The easiest way to remember ıg is to associate it with emotion. Events that are "tagged" ưtion become memories, because they are important. A gazelle that narrowly escapes a crocodile attack at a watering hole needs to remember that information, so the powerful emotion it feels will tag it as important. It gets ingrained. By using the word *love*, one of life's strongest emotions, you emotionally tag the statement, pushing it deeper into the subconscious.

(b) Positive perspective

Always phrase your affirmations positively, because your subconscious doesn't understand negatives. For your subconscious, it doesn't matter whether you use the phrase "quit smoking" or "start smoking" – it simply picks up "smoking", and that's what it will encourage your conscious mind to do.

(c) Question

You will use questions. When you create positive self-statements using strong emotion, you are well on your way to having them penetrate your subconscious. But they may still be incongruent with your deeply held beliefs, producing a struggle between the conscious and subconscious mind. You know from Chapter 4 that the subconscious will most likely win, so you need another rhetorical strategy: using a question rather than a statement.

Questions help us frame things. If you ask yourself, "Why can't I do this?", it presupposes that you can't do it, and that you have to do it. Instead, if you ask, "How can I most easily make this work?", this directs your focus differently. Here are a few ways you can phrase questions to help rather than hinder:

- What would happen if this was no longer a roadblock?
- If I knew there was a simple answer, what would it be?
- What have I not thought of yet?

Using the question format *"Why is it that...?"* therefore produces a stronger reaction and an element of inevitability that will help the affirmation to percolate.

A 2010 study by Senay and colleagues shows the effectiveness of interrogative self-talk (asking questions) versus declarative affirmations (making self-statements). Four groups were challenged to solve anagrams. Beforehand, the researchers told them they were interested in handwriting practices, and asked them to write *I will*, *Will I*, *I*, or *Will* twenty times on a sheet of paper. The group that wrote *Will I*, the interrogative, solved nearly twice as many anagrams as any other group.

Your mindset is the set of beliefs that constitutes your approach, your responses, and your interpretations of events, resulting in a movement towards or away from a vision or a goal.

(d) Present tense

Lastly, you use the present tense to instruct your subconscious that this is a fact, that it has already taken place. Your subconscious doesn't differentiate between the actual truth and an imagined truth; it accepts the idea that "that's just the way it is".

2. **Read your manual**

You will need to read your Mindset Manual each morning. Do it first thing. There is no need to answer the questions – just reading them is enough. You don't need to spend a lot of time on each question; a quick read through is fine. It should take less than ten minutes.

Don't expect a shift in mindset the first time you read the manual. It will take a little time –longer for some people, and some affirmations, than others. You may find that some don't take root and will need reworking. But the habit of reading the Mindset Manual daily and the resulting consistency are what will create deep-seated change in your mindset.

Let's write it.

It's time to fill in the Mindset Manual. Write with passion – big, bold, and easy to read!

Begin with the pilot version, and skip the first two pages – you'll need these for the complete version later. On page 3, write the following:

Why is it that I love doing my 10 steps each day?

On the opposite page, write the steps (these will all be covered in subsequent chapters):

1. *Read my manual, 10 minutes*
2. *Practise stillness, 10 minutes*

3. *Imagination, 5 minutes*
4. *Daily review, 5 minutes*
5. *Movement*
6. *Daily check-in*
7. *Fuel right*
8. *Hydration*
9. *Daily planner for the next day*
10. *Early 8*

On the next page (leaving the opposite page blank), write:

> *Why is it that I love having all the ability I need to get everything done in the day?*

On the next page (leaving the opposite page blank), write:

> *Why is it that I love writing my full to-do list for my next day in advance, from start to finish, which completely programs my subconscious mind and allows me to live my day in the flow?*

Using big, energetic, legible letters, continue by adding the following:

> *Why is it that I love doing my 10 steps five days a week, helping me to live a 10-out-of-10 day?*
> *Why is it that I love letting go of being hard on myself from this moment on, and only praising the young person that I am?*
> *Why is it that I love prioritizing, and having fun doing the priority stuff?*
> *Why is it that I love knowing that every thought that I have is a disempowering thought or an empowering thought – and from this moment on I only choose only the empowering ones?*

Why is it that I love improving by 1% each day?

Why is it that I know that everything I need lies within me?

Why is it I know that knowledge is power but is useless unless I use it every day?

Why is it I love doing each task as an exciting adventure throughout the day?

Why is it I love being number one and being a champion at everything I do?

Why is it I love releasing myself from the old baggage and living now with adventure and freedom?

Why is it that I love challenging myself with these three weekly questions:

What went great last week?

What could be even greater?

What will a 10/10 week look like for me?

Mindset manual, complete version

As well as what you have written in the pilot version, you should include the following in your complete version. On the first page, write:

Why is it that I love that I identified all my roles in life?

Now list the roles that you identified in the vision workbook. For example:

- Father
- Son
- Spouse

- Leader
- Friend

Or whatever you have come up with. Then integrate your vision statement:

> *Why is it that I love living my [insert vision statement] with conviction and clarity every day?*

Then add:

> *Why is it I love that I enjoy the journey towards my vision and that I am content at each step and live in the present moment?*

Then add:

> *Why is it that I love having all the time in the world for all my roles?*

Next, add all your relevant goals, creating one affirmation for each, on one page each, in the usual format:

> *Why is it that I love having achieved my goal of [insert goal]?*

You may not have achieved it yet, but don't tell your subconscious! Keep it in the positive, interrogative format.

Then add:

> *Why is it that I love that I [insert superpower] every day?*

Next, add each value that you need to build or work on:

> *Why is it that I love that I am a person of [insert value] and I practise it every day?*

Each year and each quarter, you can add goals that you have identified through the vision process.

I'll give you one example of how the Mindset Manual helped me this week. At the time of writing I am visiting my wife's family in Santiago for Christmas. I love her family, but I don't engage with them much. That is partly due to the language barrier, although my Spanish is improving, but mainly it's because I don't focus on it. When I'm in Santiago, I'm always working: I hire an office and go to work every day. I know that having a closer relationship with them would help my wife, my son, and myself, but I just don't make the time. Two days ago I decided to do something about it, so I took out my Mindset Manual and added:

> *Why is it that I love spotting opportunities to connect with and show appreciation for Jose, Eliana, Barbara, and Ricardo and acting on those to build strong relationships that are beneficial to the whole family?*

I wrote that on Monday, so I read it first on Tuesday morning. That evening, Jose mentioned that he liked a certain type of food, and immediately I knew what I needed to do. I had spotted an opportunity. I like the same food, so I asked Jose if there was a restaurant in Santiago that served it. He found one, and tonight we are going for dinner, just the two of us – something we have never done in the 20 years since I first met him.

All I needed was to change my mindset, and the opportunity popped up. It may seem a trivial thing, but it was very important for me. Within a couple of weeks we had done multiple things together, just the two of us, and it has strengthened our relationship.

*

In summary: If you do not build a flexible, growth-oriented mindset that is congruent with achieving your goals, you will continue to live a life dictated by your current mindset. You can develop your mindset by using affirmations in the Mindset Manual every day. The affirmations must follow a specific format: They must be interrogative, be positive, evoke emotion, and give a sense of having been achieved already. Building and implementing your Mindset Manual is easy. Just get a notebook, copy the affirmations given above, and read it daily. You will quickly see small positive changes.

In the next chapter, you will learn how to use stillness coupled with a clear vision to help you build the mindset you need for predictable success.

7. Stillness

In this chapter you will learn how to create stillness and space in your mind, enabling you to become more creative, minimize stress, and increase your focus. This will improve your energy and productivity.

Meditation is the technique you will use to create this stillness and calm. You will learn how to slow things down and will get an insight into what is going on in your mind, which will help you to manage situations every day. You will gain an understanding of the power of meditation and how it fits into the Game Changer Formula.

> *If you correct your mind, the rest of your life will fall into place.*
> —Lao Tzu

I like to compare meditation to exercise. Meditation is like a gym for your mind – but where the body benefits from movement in the gym, the mind benefits from stillness. Physical exercise at the gym is focused: you use different exercises for different muscle groups. Over time, you get better at those exercises and you build strength.

Meditation is similar. There are different exercises and focuses by which you develop different parts of the mind and enhance different areas of your life. It is difficult to see the results after one session, but over time you will build mind muscle and see improvements across many aspects of your life.

To meditate is to clear the mind of distractions as much as possible and to try to maintain one clear focus. You will use meditation as part of the Game Changer Formula to build the strength of mind you need to support your journey to the life you deserve.

Meditation helps you achieve this through developing a calm mind that can deal effectively with things that don't go your way. It helps you develop skills that allow you to acknowledge issues, deal with them in an appropriate and relaxed way, and not let them affect your mindset.

As you embark on the journey towards your Power Vision, you will encounter many distractions and obstacles. You will need to develop the focus and concentration to be productive every day, and to learn how to deal with distractions that pull your attention away from your priorities.

> Meditation is like a gym for your mind – but whereas the body benefits from movement in the gym, the mind benefits from stillness.

Creating stillness in your mind through daily meditation will:

- give you the ability to create clarity around your goals and objectives, which will make decision-making quicker, clearer, and more effective

- help you to relax, rejuvenating your mind and body and giving you more energy to dedicate to your vision

- help you deal with stress and anxiety, which will empower you to overcome the inevitable bumps that appear in your path

- help you develop a more creative mind for solving problems and finding new paths

- help you develop patience, acceptance, and understanding, improving your relationships at work and at home

- help you deal with change, both internally and externally

- build resilience that will empower you to make better decisions along your journey.

In general, it will make you a happier, healthier, stronger, and more open and accepting person, with better capacity to take on the world and not succumb to its pressures.

Meditation has been in use, and its benefits understood, for thousands of years. Recent studies have shown that it can rewire neural connections in the brain. Our capacity of neuroplasticity means that change occurs in brain structure and organization through experiences, learnings, and adaptations.

With each new thought, you begin to create a new way of being. With each repetition of that thought, you strengthen the neural pathway until it becomes like a well-trodden path through the wood. These small changes, when repeated often enough, lead to changes in how your brain works.

> Ship's Log: Nov. 27 – No position logged.
>
> Last night was crystal clear and the stars shone brightly. The phosphorescence glowed blue-green from under the hull, but astern it created the appearance of a minute electrical storm, fireworking continually. We have the usual small particles, but once every couple of seconds a mini underwater explosion of light shines through, sometimes quite delayed, 15 metres behind.
>
> We create two wakes of light, one the rudder and the second the towed water generator as *Cerys* caresses the surface of the Atlantic. We are enjoying the show tonight, just me and Iggy Pop. As I change to the Smashing Pumpkins the phosphorescence seems more choreographed. Plenty of time to think, listen to music, and watch the stars. There is little or no traffic to worry about.
>
> The simplicity of life out here means that I am far more aware of my thoughts and more present with my surroundings. We miss so much stuff in life, being busy.

Meditation can sound daunting at first, but it doesn't have to be. I am not an expert, but I have done hundreds of short sessions, and I know how the 80:20 rule works.

> *The goal of meditation is not to get rid of thoughts or emotions. The goal is to become more aware of your thoughts and emotions and learn how to move through them without getting stuck.* —Dr. Philippe Goldin

Let's take it in simple steps. To begin, It's good to find a quiet space where you won't be distracted. Sometimes that's easier said than done. For me it's the kitchen at ten to six in the morning, before anyone is up. Try to find a particular space that you can meditate in at the same time each day, creating a strong habit. You will need somewhere to sit.

Next, decide how long you want to meditate for. For the Daily 10, I suggest 10 minutes; that's what I practise. It is better to meditate five days for 10 minutes a day than one day for 50 minutes.

Sit comfortably and symmetrically, on a chair or the floor, with your arms and legs uncrossed. Your arms can be by your side or on your lap, and your posture should be strong but not tense. If you're in a chair, keep your feet flat on the floor. I use a cushion to support my lower back, but do whatever is comfortable for you.

I suggest using guided meditation to begin. There are many YouTube videos you can use, but I recommend the Headspace meditation app. It costs $8–13 a month, but you will make that back many times in focus, productivity, and composure. Start with The Basics course and you can graduate from there.

If you want to begin right now, try this body scan technique. Close your eyes. Starting at the top of your head, mentally scan all the way down through your body. Notice which parts feel relaxed or tense, comfortable or uncomfortable, light or heavy. Don't try to change any of them – just be aware. This should take around 20 seconds.

Run the scan a few times, and use observations to build a mental image of how your body feels right now. When thoughts arise, simply return to the area of the body where you last left off. Don't worry – thoughts will arise. It's normal. Once you've practised this technique and feel comfortable with it, try a more in-depth meditation.

You will find that your mind will not sit still. All sorts of thoughts will jump in. That's what the mind does. Meditation is not about stopping thoughts: it's about observing without engaging. You will learn over time how to train your mind to become aware when it wanders and calmly bring it back to your focus, which may be the body scan, your breath, or a visualization.

Occasionally you'll reach a point of complete stillness, but don't be worried if it takes a while. (Sometimes time will play tricks on you: ten minutes can feel like one or twenty.) Suddenly, self-chatter can be cleared away; stress and confusion disappear. Your priorities become apparent, your thoughts slow, and you find space for ideas, creativity, and new ways of thinking.

In time, your mind will become comfortable with stillness, and you will begin to use this new skill throughout your day to work towards achieving your vision.

In the Headspace app, you will find meditation practices for just about anything: stress, sport, anxiety, sleep, food, happiness, health. One that I love is the kids' practices. Each morning before school, my seven-year-old son and I lie on the soft mat in his play area. He chooses a kids' meditation and we do it together. Some involve placing a favourite toy on your chest as a way to become aware of your breathing. My son fidgets a bit and doesn't always want to do it. But I see it as laying down a track and starting to form a habit that for him will become a key tool in developing his potential as a human being.

When you begin, build a slow and steady approach to meditation. The morning practice allows your brain to learn at its own pace how to be open and present, and you will be able to extend that awareness into your everyday life. With continued practice you will also notice that you become more confident with your meditation. That will be helpful some days when things are just not working out as planned.

Sometimes meditation works better for me than other times. I need to practise a lot more, but I have noticed that it has improved my ability to focus on difficult tasks for longer. I am less easily distracted. It has reduced my stress levels significantly – stress doesn't really affect me anymore, and meditation played a large part in that, but it was also helped by the Mindset Manual, exercise, and the Daily Planner.

I am much calmer now when dealing with difficult situations. Patience, which was non-existent for me before, is now a strong point. I know there are many other changes in me that can be accredited to meditation, but it's sometimes difficult to put your finger on them. Meditation takes only ten minutes a day, but it is adding immeasurable happiness to my life and the lives of people around me.

If you think you don't have time for ten minutes of meditation, consider Mahatma Gandhi when he was trying to drive a colonial power out of India and keep Hindus and Muslims from slaughtering each other. At the beginning of a particularly busy day, Gandhi said, "I have so much to accomplish today that I must meditate for two hours instead of one."

In time, you will become so comfortable with meditation that you will be able to do it anywhere. I can now run through quick flashes of my morning meditation while at my desk, in a queue, or stuck in traffic. One friend meditates in car parks or shopping malls while waiting for his wife or kids, who never show up on time!

*

In summary: Meditation is a powerful life tool that fits into the mindset element of the Game Changer Formula, along with visualization, the Mindset Manual, and the Daily Review. Practising it every morning will give you many skills you can use to navigate your way to your vision. Those skills work with both body and mind. Start your meditation journey simply by getting the Headspace meditation app and starting with "The Basics".

In the next chapter, we step into our imagination. This is an essential constituent of the Game Changer Formula and will help you to achieve what you truly want out of life.

8. Imagination

In this chapter you will learn how to use your imagination to visualize your goals with a simple technique. You will understand why this is part of the Daily 10 and the Game Changer Formula.

We are what we believe. —C. S. Lewis

Visualization is the use of your imagination to create pictures or mental images that represent what you want to achieve. It is a powerful tool to help you realize your vision. It can help you to improve yourself and identify opportunities and structures for achieving your goals.

Visualization supports your Mindset Manual in developing your mindset. The manual focuses on affirmations, which can take time to penetrate, but visualization penetrates immediately.

People often use visualization to develop their sporting skills, picturing themselves striking a ball, receiving a medal, swimming in a particular time, or knocking out a boxing opponent.

Using visualization as a preparation technique leads to better performance and results. This is true in sport, business, and life. Michael Phelps, who has won more Olympic medals than anyone in history, uses visualization twice a day to achieve his goals. His coach, Bob Bowman, instructs him to watch a "mental videotape" of his races before going to sleep and again when he wakes up. Phelps visualizes every aspect of swimming a successful race, starting from the blocks and culminating in a celebration after he wins the race.

Visualization will help you work towards predictable success by developing your mindset for success and giving you a clear direction every day. It will reduce stress and give you a focal point that keeps you on track to your Power Vision.

You will learn to take your attention away from what you don't want, and to focus on what you deserve to happen in your life. Visualization will focus your attention on actions that enable you to achieve predictable success. The more detailed your visualization, the better it will work.

Visualization works by creating the illusion in your subconscious that the image or event you're visualizing is reality. If you vividly visualize a future situation, complete with emotions and all the senses, your mind will save it as a real memory. The image will become known, something you've already experienced. It is much easier to do something the second time around. You will feel confident in your ability to go through the situation, because you will already have done it successfully.

> Visualization works by creating the illusion in your subconscious that the image or event visualized is reality.

You will notice that you encounter more opportunities that are congruent with you achieving your goals. This is because of what's called our reticular activating system, located at the base of the brain. Our brains are overloaded with constant messages. We are exposed to millions of pieces of information a day: words, sounds, tastes, images, feelings, and much more.

It's far too much for the brain to process, so we evolved the reticular activating system as a filter. It filters out what is mostly irrelevant to us, so we process only what it deems important. That's why when we learn a new word, we start to hear it everywhere. It's why we can hear our own name whispered across a crowded room. It's amazing how it works.

Because of this filter, your brain looks for things that corroborate its beliefs and ideas. So you can use visualization as a tool to modify the filter. Just like the subconscious, you can train your reticular activating system to work for you and advance you on the journey towards your Power Vision. You can program the filter so it allows the right things through – things like opportunities that could lead you to predictable success.

There are six steps to visualization:

1. Know what you want
2. Know why you want it
3. Describe your vision
4. Begin the visualization
5. Wrap up
6. Give thanks

1. Know what you want

Go through the Power Vision process and workbook so you know what to visualize. If you haven't done that yet, don't worry. It's important to get started, so choose a short-term goal that you already know you want to achieve, and visualize that. Later you can change your visualization to work with your Power Vision.

2. Know why you want it

A simple reason is good. So, for example, you could just enjoy the visualization the first few times you do it. After that, you may want to discover your focus for the day ahead, or the priorities you need to work on to ensure you stay on the road to your vision.

3. Describe your vision

Picture the subject of your visualization – what you want to achieve – in as much detail as you can. Clarity is key! Ask yourself, "If I had a magic wand and could create the life I want, the life in my vision, what would it look like?"

When visualizing, it is important to see things in your mind not as a spectator but from your own point of view, through your own eyes. Picture the position you will be in once you attain your goal. Notice the fine details, the colours, smells, textures, temperature, the people around you. Figure out what emotions you will experience. Images that are bigger, brighter, and bolder have more emotional intensity, making your practice more valuable.

Athletes don't just hope they win gold: they set themselves up for it. Katie Taylor began programming herself for Olympic gold in women's boxing at seven years old. At that age she practised receiving her medal on the podium even though women's boxing was not yet an Olympic sport. She had to fight first to make it an Olympic sport and then fight for the gold medal she knew was hers.

Write your vision down, or create a vision board to support you the first few times. After that, it will become natural.

4. Begin the visualization

When you are ready to begin, try to find a quiet place where you won't be interrupted. Put your phone on silent, and just start. Once you practise a little, you'll be able to do it anywhere, any time, but it's much easier to learn it in a quiet environment.

Now visualize the outcome you've described – the sights, sounds, even the taste. This is your reality for these few minutes. Experiencing the emotions of having achieved your result is very important, so that you identify with the vision and make it part of who you are. You may find this difficult at first, but in time you will perfect it in your own way. Try to see the image through your own eyes in the practice. It is the future you who is experiencing this, so you must see it as a participant, not as an observer of yourself.

As the images come to you and the emotions run, the visualization becomes clearer. It's like having a foggy window: On one side is a clear image of what you are trying to see, and on the other side is you. As you practise visualizing, the foggy window becomes clearer. It can take time. You are trying to clear that fog and create your own film of your future life.

5. Wrap up

As you finish your short visualization session, ask yourself what you can take from the experience and bring into your day. In the beginning, this may also be difficult, but you will get better at it.

6. Give thanks

Thank yourself for taking the time to practise your visualization.

Visualization alone will not bring you magically to a place where you achieve all your goals. You need to work at achieving those goals. You need to commit and follow a structure – that's why visualization is one tenth of the daily routine. But it is an important tenth.

A goal believed becomes a goal achieved. In time, you will visualize when exercising, waiting for a train, even taking a one-minute break at work.

Visualization may look like meditation, but they are two distinct things – though they complement each other. There can be visualization in meditation, but for our purposes here it's best to consider them separate steps.

There are hundreds of definitions of meditation, so I will make a simple distinction for you (though some will see it differently): Meditation is clearing the mind of distractions as much as you can and attempting to maintain one clear focus. Visualization is filling the mind with one clear picture and its associated sensations.

Some people find visualization difficult. You may think you cannot visualize at all, but your difficulty is most likely just an inability to visualize on demand. Everyone dreams, and dreams are visualizations, so you have the ability. You just need some practice to develop it. If you find it tough to visualize images or a movie, or you only get words, or emotions don't come to you, that's not a failure. It just takes practice.

Every time you imagine your vision, that's visualization, so just keep at it. You may need to try a little harder or more regularly than some people, but you may be better than them at other steps in the Daily 10.

You can also try the lemon visualization exercise. Imagine there's a bowl of lemons in front of you. You reach out and choose a ripe yellow lemon. You feel its weight in your hand, you touch its skin with your fingertips, and you sense the tiny dimples, the waxiness, the coolness, the rough ends. Now raise the lemon to your face and breathe in that lemony scent. Feel it as it enters your nostrils and chokes the senses just a little. Now slice the lemon open. Some tiny lemon drops hit your face and enter your mouth and nose. As the bright yellow flesh is exposed, you see the juice run out. You cut a slice and put it into your mouth. As you bite, the juice runs around your tongue. Inside your cheeks, your mouth fills with the bitter taste of lemon juice…

Having done this exercise, most people salivate. Did you? If so, your body has responded with a powerful reflex. It shows you that visualization can have a physical impact on the body.

Visualization is a technique I applied for years without knowing what it was. I wanted to sail across the Atlantic and live on a boat in the Caribbean for years. It was just an idea that lingered in my mind, but I could not act on it, as my business took up most of my life. There was also the small matter of not knowing how to sail.

One night I had dinner with a guy called Jamie Young, an adventurer. When I brought up my idea of sailing, he answered with a short phrase: "Just do it." That made me realize the conflict that existed within me. I wanted this idea to happen, but I was telling myself it never would. I had a great excuse.

From that moment on, I started thinking not of *how* I would do it but of what I would look like crossing the Atlantic. I started to see an image of me doing it, feeling the salty air, my boat plunging through the water. I felt the fear of mid-Atlantic storms, and I dreamt about the minute details of the boat and my equipment.

In a notebook I drew how my boat would look, how big and comfortable it would be, how well it would manage rough seas. Most of what I drew and considered was ridiculous, because I knew nothing about boats. I was mainly concerned with having a bed you could get out of on either side, so that my wife and I would be comfortable. I can only laugh at that now.

Back then I wasn't aware that what I was doing was a kind of visualization: my notebook with all the crazy details, spending every spare minute thinking through various scenarios in images. That process pulled me through to reality. It opened up opportunities that I would otherwise have been blind to. I began reading books about solo transatlantic sailors, boats capsizing in the Southern Ocean, and the off-water challenges all these sailors faced before even launching a boat. Through all this I was learning, and I didn't even know it.

In 2008 I sold my business, and six weeks later my wife and I bought a sailboat. It had a bed you could only access from one side. We also realized they are called bunks. We learned how to sail and navigate and did all the survival-at-sea training. We learned how to make repairs, how to generate power, and what gear to prepare.

In May 2008 we packed up and sailed off. We ended up living on that boat for two years, sailing from Ireland along the coast of Europe, across the Atlantic to the Caribbean. Our plan was to sell the boat after that adventure, but then some friends wanted to sail across the Atlantic too, so we set off again and sailed back to Europe.

I never thought my epic idea could ever happen, but with the power of visualization, it did.

Here is how I visualize today. Jim, my coach, wanted me to visualize several distinct goals I had written, for my business, family, health, and mental attitude. Initially I visualized by creating four distinct images, one for each goal. I found it hard to jump from one to the next in my session each morning. It just didn't feel right. It can work for some people, but it needs to feel right for you.

One Friday afternoon I took time out and went for a long walk with my notebook, drawing and writing different scenarios. I was trying to consolidate all these goals into one, but it was difficult to get something logical – and I'm a pretty logical person. How could I get my entire vision into one image or set of images?

I had read about people visualizing their funeral and what people would say about them. I understood the concept, but it didn't feel right to me to visualize my death, especially since one of my goals is to live to at least 120. I decided instead to visualize my 100th birthday. So now what I visualize each morning is the following:

I am at the dinner table in Ballynahinch Castle, a hotel on the west coast of Ireland. My table is near the fire, and I am surrounded by my close family. At the other tables are my close friends, my business partners, people I have helped throughout my life, and some charities I support financially. The closer a person is seated to me, the more important they are to me, so my wife is beside me. But my son's chair on my other side is empty.

I smell the wood burning in the fire, and I see the way it has turned grey like an elephant's skin. I taste the warm wine; there are a few drops on the tablecloth. I feel the coarse texture of the napkin. I see what I'm wearing by looking down at myself – it is me; I'm not looking at myself from a distance.

I feel people as they walk past and touch my shoulder. There is a mild smell in the air of the dinner that has been cleared away. Because I've already written the guest list for this party, I know who's there. My son's chair is empty because he is standing in front of everyone, about to make a speech. As the room falls silent, apart from some coughs, laughter, whispers, and clinks of glasses and cutlery, I can hear the hiss of the wood fire.

My son begins by complaining that he didn't get to write his speech until three in the morning. I wouldn't go to bed until two because I was having too much *craic* in the bar and he needed to talk to my friends and work partners to get stories for his speech. (*Craic*, or *crack*, is used a lot in Ireland to describe fun or enjoyment. But it's more than that: it commonly refers to a good night out, often with alcohol or music.)

He complains, jokingly, about his inheritance, with a wink at me across the room. That's because I have just given a big sum of money to charity. The wink is because earlier that day I also transferred substantial assets to him. Both amounts are defined. The room laughs, and everyone gets the joke, and I am proud of how he holds the room.

Today, as I write this, he is seven years old.

His speech is about the various roles I have played in my hundred years. He says I have been the best father I could have been, the best husband, friend, leader, and so on. He talks about how I am still childlike at a hundred, still learning every day, still teaching every day. He says I seem younger and fitter now than before. He describes my different projects and their success in making money and helping people. He talks about how I have impacted the lives of about 100,000 people. That's the number he and my friends and colleagues agreed on at three AM. Then he presents me with a piece of art that is too involved and personal to discuss here, but it represents the fact that I changed those 100,000 lives for the better.

My son's speech brings many emotions to me as I visualize it. The details are clear: I know the faces in the room; I know who is at each table. It's an intimate, warm, and exciting event. When he finishes, there are a lot of hugs. The DJ comes on and plays *Billie Jean* and we all dance like crazy. Today I don't like dancing, at all, but I want to see and feel that I can do that at one hundred.

Along with meditation, visualization will stimulate your mind to focus on thoughts and actions that lead you in your intended direction. To visualize, you need a clear vision of what you want to achieve. Visualization itself is simple, but it may take a little practice. The more detail and emotion you can bring to the image, the better it will serve you.

*

In summary: The steps to visualization are: know what you want, decide why you are visualizing, describe it in detail, create your mental image using your imagination, feel it, learn something from it, and thank yourself.

In the next chapter, you will learn how to use the simple Daily Review to extract lessons from each day and implement them. This will result in daily compound improvement that can make you 37 times better than you are today.

9. The Daily Review

In this chapter you will discover a short, simple process that you can use daily to ensure you learn and improve by 1 per cent each day, leading to compound improvement.

> *Learn from yesterday, live for today, hope for tomorrow.* — Anonymous

The fourth part of the Daily 10 is the Daily Review. This is a tool to help you implement continuous evaluation and development every day. You will learn how each day can be better than the last, and how to compound that growth throughout the year.

If you could make a 1 per cent improvement each day, that would mean a 37-times improvement after one year. From one day to the next, that degree of progression is barely perceptible, but at the end of a year it's enormous.

The Daily Review takes just five minutes a day. Using it, you will:

- realize your strengths
- structure your day better
- avoid repeating things that are not helping you to achieve your goal
- get your own outside perspective on your activity

- take soundings and change course when needed
- identify the one element you can work on developing each day
- concentrate on self-evaluation
- identify any weaknesses
- understand what you do well
- figure out what you could do better
- learn how to improve.

The Daily Review is a way to debrief the preceding day. You identify what you could do better, and you use that to form a better today. It involves three simple "what" questions:

1. What went great yesterday?
2. What could have gone better?
3. What do I need to do today to make it a 10-out-of-10 day?

It is important to use the questions in this order, because starting with the positive will allow you to be more open to realizing and identifying what could have gone better.

There are many more questions you could ask, to reveal more detail and improve even further. But remember the 80:20 rule. Too much information can produce paralysis or procrastination. You only need to improve by 1 per cent, so keep it simple and brief.

> If you could make a 1 per cent improvement each day, that would mean a 37-times improvement after one year.

Each day just after your visualization, spend five minutes analyzing the preceding day. Start from when you woke up, and go through the day in your mind from sleep to sleep. As a prompt to get started, consider the following:

Did you get up on time?
Did you complete your Daily 10?
How was your nutrition at breakfast and lunch?
How did you interact with your family over breakfast?
Were you present throughout the day?
When you walked in the door at work, what was on your mind?
How did you interact with colleagues throughout the day?
Did you get into your Daily Planner immediately, or did you start with emails?
Did you maintain productivity throughout the day?
Did you hydrate throughout the day?
Did you listen as much as you could have?
Did you complete your Daily Planner?
Did you get out of work on time?
Did you prepare tomorrow's Daily Planner?
Did you make a clean break between work and home?
Were you focused on your home role as you walked in the door?
Did you meet your family where they were?
Did you eat a healthy dinner?
Did you try to understand?
Did you get to bed on time?

This may seem like a long list, but it should only take a minute or two. Then recap all these elements, and ask yourself what you could have done better.

Do the Daily Review each day after your visualization. From what you did well and what could have been better, choose one to three items that you could either continue to do today or change up to make this a 10-out-of-10 day. That's enough to ensure you are on a compound improvement trajectory.

Take those few things and write them into your Daily Planner in the "Today's Focus" section (see Chapter 11). Some days there may be nothing suitable, and that's okay; Today's Focus can come from multiple sources, as you'll see.

When I do the Daily Review right after visualizing, I just stay put, close my eyes, and go through the previous day chronologically. This way I can examine everything that happened from the time I woke up to the time I went to bed: family, work, and the rest. I assess what went great and what I could have done better, then I ask myself what a 10-out-of-10 day would be for me today.

Here's an example.

What went great yesterday?

Exercise was great – I felt energetic throughout the day. I had a healthy breakfast and lunch. When I got to work, I wasted no time, getting to my Daily Planner immediately and starting with the highest-priority task…

Then I review the activities of the work day and consider each one. I review the communications I had with people throughout the day. Did I listen? Did I judge? Did I dismiss? Did I consume my target intake of water in the day? I left work at a reasonable time. I got to spend time with my son and concentrated on his world for a while. I had a productive evening, with no television, and I went to bed on time.

What could have gone better?

When I reviewed my Daily Planner, it didn't look like a high-pressure day, so instead of pushing hard through the morning, I took it easy, which meant I was under pressure to accomplish everything in the afternoon. I could have eaten a healthier dinner (I could have easily avoided the French fries.) When I got home after work, I should have had complete focus on home and not carried work with me through the door.

What could I do better to have a 10-out-of-10 day today?

Under Today's Focus, put "kick the day off hard" – even if it looks like an easy day. That way I may get out of work earlier. Turn off my phone for an hour before I walk in the front door at home. Take a minute before entering, to clear my mind of work and concentrate on my role as husband and father. Do this by taking ten breaths and focusing on the role ahead as I come in the gate.

It is important not to be hard on yourself with the things that could have gone better. Sometimes your subconscious mind can be surprisingly harsh on you. You probably wouldn't be that hard on someone else. All you are trying to do is improve by 1 per cent each day. Things will go wrong – it happens all the time. Learn from it and move on.

You can take this a step further with a weekly review, if you wish. On Friday or Sunday evening, review what took place during the week. The three questions are similar:

1. What went great last week?
2. What could have gone better?
3. What do I need to do this week to make it a 10-out-of-10 week?

Use exactly the same process. Reviewing the week can reveal patterns that may require change. For example, you may realize that you're not listening as intently as you should. A weekly review often highlights areas that require work through your subconscious and should therefore be added to the Mindset Manual. If your productivity often declines after lunch, for example, add an affirmation to your manual to reverse that pattern: *Why is it that I love being even more productive after lunch than I am in the morning?*

Using these three simple questions every day and every week will ensure you are self-assessing and progressing continuously, creating compound improvement across all aspects of your life. If you did only this and nothing else for a year, imagine how your life could change for the better.

*

In summary: Using three simple questions daily to review the previous day, then acting on the results, will ensure you are improving every day, leading to compound improvement that will drive you towards predictable success faster than you would imagine.

In the next chapter, you will see why accountability is crucial to success, and how a simple daily text message can change your life.

10. The Daily Check-In

You will now learn how to stay on track every day to achieve your lifetime goal. You will understand why this is important, how to set it up, and what kind of person you should have as an accountability partner.

> *Accountability separates the wishers in life from the action-takers that care enough about their future to account for their daily actions.*
> —John Di Lemme

As part of the Daily 10, you will check in with an accountability partner to help you stay on track. You are doing everything possible to keep up your daily routine by ensuring it is ingrained in your subconscious and becomes part of who you are.

Nothing replaces persistence – not genius, not talent, not planning, not even a great idea. Having an accountability partner to check in with ensures that you persist. This persistence is essential for the "predictable" part of predictable success. You need accountability for two reasons:

1. It takes a little while to train your subconscious, and you need to ensure you don't falter in that initial period.

2. Having someone else's perspective on your activity ensures that nothing falls through the cracks that may appear. Nobody is perfect, so you need a process to ensure you are on track every single day.

Do not skip this step, even if you think you will be okay. Prioritize it.

Accountability accelerates your performance. When you are accountable to someone, the thought of embarrassing yourself by admitting you have not followed through means you get every step done every day.

The Daily 10 in the Game Changer process succeeds because it is a routine built on a defined goal. The more times you check every box on the Daily 10, the faster you will reach your true goal. People with an accountability partner are much more likely to achieve their goals, because what gets measured gets done – and what gets measured and reported on *always* gets done.

Checking in daily also keeps you engaged. When you contact your partner each day, you become more engaged in your activity. Just knowing you need to report on it makes you more connected with your daily activity.

Accountability will keep you responsible. You answer to yourself, but being answerable to someone else creates more responsibility around your actions and goals. You are far less likely to blame outside factors for failure.

It will also validate your thoughts, ideas, and plans. A good accountability partner will sanity-check these to ensure you are doing what's best to reach your goals. They should keep you grounded in reality. It's easy to get sidetracked by an incongruent goal or to drift onto a fantasy track. Having a partner will keep it real. Getting that honest feedback is invaluable. If you need an outside opinion, and you don't have an accountability partner who understands what you are doing, you may have a hard time getting a valid opinion.

With an accountability partner, you will be forced to set firm deadlines for important tasks. To make a decision, you need to decide, put a date on it, then tell someone. Your partner solves the third step. You will be under observation, and people perform better in those circumstances. When you know you are being watched, the parts of the brain associated with social awareness and reward invigorate your motor skills, improving your performance.

> People with an accountability partner are 80–95% more likely to achieve their goals.

As a bonus, you will have someone to share your success with. Working towards your vision can be lonely, especially if you haven't shared your goals and plans with the people around you. You may have reasons not to do so, and that's fine, but it's great to have an accountability partner to share your wins with – both big and small.

How your accountability partner should help you

Each day, your accountability partner should expect a check-in from you by a certain time – ideally before ten AM. That gives you time to fix any issue if you need to. You can check in by phone, text, email, or in person. Some people use a Google Sheet, a Trello board, or an app like stickK. Your message should simply inform your partner that you are on track with your Daily 10 – something like "I'm on track for today, Bill. 10/10. Thanks for the help." Short, sweet, and to the point.

Your accountability partner should have a reminder on their phone so that if they have not heard from you by the agreed time, they should message you to see if everything is okay and on track. They are not a slave driver: they should not berate you if something has gone off track. That's actually counterproductive.

On a weekly basis, you should send your accountability partner your 10-out-of-10 week from your Weekly Review (Chapter 9). Do this on Monday and ask them to check in with you on Friday to ensure you covered them all and to briefly discuss any issues.

How do you find an accountability partner? The best solution for most people is to ask a friend or colleague. You need to find someone who is open and able to check in with you daily. If possible, find someone more disciplined than you. Not only will they be reliable, but some of that discipline may rub off on you.

Choose a person who is challenging but non-judgemental. You will need a compassionate challenge from time to time, but if your partner keeps judging you and being negative, it's time to change. Your spouse or partner is not ideal for this role – you are just too close.

Choose a partner you would hate to disappoint. Some people generate more discomfort if you have to tell them you didn't follow through. They make great accountability partners. It should be someone with a positive mindset, and ideally someone who asks great and sometimes difficult questions.

An ideal partner is someone who understands how powerful the Game Changer Daily 10 is. This may be someone who has read this book or has their own daily routine that includes a few elements of the Daily 10. Find a partner who has the time to invest in your goals. If they don't, it won't work out. That will quickly become apparent.

You could try multiple partners. Two or three can work well: one for the morning, one for the evening, and one for a weekly check-in, for example. A coach or mentor could also be a good option, if you find one who feels like a good fit. See roryprendergast.com for options to work with me or Jim on accountability.

How to choose the right person

Make a shortlist of potential partners, and list their characteristics that could be advantageous or disadvantageous. Select two and meet them for a coffee or call them. Use the Accountability Partner Scripts you will find in Chapter 23.

Start with two partners. Share your vision with them. Share your Daily 10, and explain what you have learned from the Game Changer Formula. Ask them if they would agree to commit on a trial basis for two weeks to see how it goes. Here are some things to bear in mind:

- Decide on the norms together.

- Own your lapses. Don't blame anyone or anything else.

- Honour your appointment times, and ask them to honour theirs.

- Customize your accountability reporting to match your goals, relationship, and time.

- Tell your new allies how to challenge you, and accept the challenge positively.

- One size does not fit all – you may need to tweak things a little.

- They don't have to be in the same city.

- Hold them accountable by telling them you are relying on them and how important this process is.
- Be consistent and respectful with them, and ask them to do the same.

- Be open and honest. Tell your partner anything you would like to do differently.

- Acknowledge that it is a commitment on their part, and consider what you can do for them in exchange. Maybe they also need accountability or something else you can help with.

- Let them have time off when on vacation, but ensure you have a backup plan.

- If things are not working out after two weeks, go back to your list.

Accountability can work against you in certain circumstances, so be careful. When an accountability partner puts you under pressure for a skill or activity you are familiar with, it has been shown to work well. When they put you under pressure for something you have not yet mastered, you could fail.

If you falter while learning, your partner should give constructive feedback. Ensure that you both clearly understand this, and allow for a learning process and a period for you to get comfortable with your new daily activities.

I believe that having a live accountability partner who knows you well, respects you, and challenges you is the best way to ensure success from an accountability review. Either that or a professional.

Non-professional accountability partners can fall by the wayside. This is natural, but it is your sole responsibility to ensure you have an accountability partner and a process that works. That's another good reason to have two partners. Be prepared to move and improve.

There are other ways of achieving something close:

- Use an app like stickK – it helps you set a goal and stay on track with a financial incentive. If you fail, you have to pay. That payment can go to a charity you'd rather not support, because of your beliefs.

- Join an accountability group. I am currently testing small groups of up to ten people to keep each other on track using an online system. If it works well, I will roll it out for more people to use.

- If you think you would benefit from having one of my team work with you on accountability, just let us know here www.roryprendergast.com/coaching. Bear in mind that there will be a charge to cover the cost of this.

- Coaching with Jim or me. We are open to helping a handful of people through one-on-one coaching and accountability by phone, messaging apps, or video calls. You would need to meet certain criteria for our coaching programme. Let us know if you are interested in applying. We also have one-off, one-on-one coaching sessions available from time to time. Contact us here to find out more www.roryprendergast.com.

Here is an observation from a business owner who is accountable to me daily:

> *Accountability to me has held my feet to the fire. It has enabled me to do more with my day, as I know someone is going to follow up. It has helped me greatly with keeping focus on my goals and not getting distracted. You have reminded me on occasions during a week what I had stated earlier as my goals/to-do list. This was a tad embarrassing. However, it showed how easily I was getting distracted with urgent but unimportant items.*

One stormy morning, I was supposed to run my usual five kilometres, with a swim in the icy Atlantic halfway through. The weather was unbelievably bad. I thought maybe I should do something else, a shorter run or the run but not the swim, but I also thought of having to tell Jim I did not do my full routine.

So I went out and ran. Normally I would pass by dozens of other runners, but that morning I passed only one. I went for my swim, which would normally be with thirty or thirty-five other people in the sea. That morning there were only two.

The fact that I got my morning routine done despite the rain made me feel really powerful, and I looked forward to the whole day, which was extremely productive. Ever since then, I relish the bad days. I know that very few other people have the resolve to run and swim in the ocean on those days. When I do, it gives me even more energy, I take energy from the wind, the cold, and the rain.

*

In summary: Accountability is the safety net of the Daily 10. If you want to ensure success, then you absolutely need it. Checking in daily with a partner will ensure you stay engaged, keep you grounded, and give you someone to share success with.

Choose an accountability partner carefully – in fact, choose two. At some point you may need to trade in your accountability partner for another model.

In the next chapter I will show you the Daily Planner. This tool ensures that your week scores 10 out of 10 and that your days flow with ease and calm.

11. The Daily Planner

The Daily Planner is the hub that connects all the moving parts of the Game Changer Formula. Everything feeds into it, directly or indirectly. In this chapter you will learn what the Daily Planner is, how it works, and how to build it out every day and every week.

> *Tomorrow belongs to the people who prepare for it today.*
> —African proverb

You know what it's like: There are just too many small things to get done during the day. Stuff for work, for home, for the kids, and for yourself. Next thing you know, it's eleven at night and you've forgotten to answer that email, pick up the dry cleaning, or get things for the kids' school lunch. Now you are going to bed stressed, and that will affect your night's sleep, which will affect your entire day tomorrow.

Let's look at how to fix this once and for all.

You need to write things down to keep track. When you write everything down on paper, you relieve your brain of trying to remember everything, freeing it up to analyze, prioritize, and process other things. By generating your list the evening before, your mind begins pre-planning, breaking tasks down, and evaluating the next day's activity.

I have tried multiple ways of working with to-do lists. I have used Trello, Asana, Evernote, phone notes, emails to myself, calendars, voice recording, a VA, and everything in between. They all worked to a certain extent, but none of them made me more productive or reduced stress sustainably. That's why I use this Daily Planner.

> Ship's Log: May 13 – Position 32:51N 50:00W – Wind SE Force 5, Full Sail, 5.3 knots, 062 degrees True
>
> We have a daily routine even outside our watches. I have delegated some of the monitoring, leaving me more time to concentrate on other things. Joey is taking care of provisions and managing our three banks of batteries, making sure each is charged in rotation and that we don't drop below critical limits. He is also plotting our positions daily on the paper charts. David monitors levels in the engine daily, along with fan belt and other checks. He changed the impeller before departure and checks the bilges daily for water. Tom is looking after sails and rigging, checking everything daily. All these daily mundane and easily forgettable tasks are critically important. Any sequence of things going wrong could put our lives in danger.
>
> Might have to dip a little bit south of a depression just ahead of us if winds look too strong on forecast this afternoon.

The Daily Planner is a simple pen-and-paper method for ensuring you get through your to-do list and progress towards your long-term goals every day. It's about process and structure. Trust me on using pen and paper over digital – give it a while and you'll see the difference.

Handwriting is an ideomotor (idea + motor) action that creates a connection between the hand and the mind. Because of this, what we write by hand, particularly in cursive (joined characters) or script, is an avenue into the subconscious. Cursive writing is free-flowing, like our thoughts, and therefore accesses the subconscious more effectively.

When all elements pull together through this hub, you generate predictable success.

The reason we want to access the subconscious is that we want that part of the mind to work while we rest the conscious mind.

As part of the Daily 10, you will fill out your Daily Planner each evening for the following day. Write up Monday's plan on Sunday, and so on. The Daily Planner integrates all elements of the Game Changer Formula. It enables all the elements to pull together through this hub, empowering you to generate predictable success.

Here is why the Daily Planner is so successful:

- gets everything down on paper
- focuses you on the priority tasks
- ensures you are working on all aspects of your vision
- switches off work mode in the evening
- puts your subconscious to work for you
- eliminates morning stress or panic
- gives you a great feeling of accomplishment
- enables accountability
- creates order
- gives you back time
- breaks down goals

- helps you visualize your day
- ensures you are working on the highest-value jobs
- integrates all elements of the Game Changer Formula.

Getting set up

You will need a second notebook for this. I find a four-by-eight-inch spiral notebook works best, as it lies flat on my desk and is easy to write on. You want something with a reasonably strong cover, as it will get a lot of use. I use the Pukka Pad brand.

Open a double page, and split the right into two panes as shown in the diagram. Write tomorrow's day and date on the first page. Each day's work or tasks will be spread across two pages. This is the anatomy of the Daily Planner. Now you will see how to build out each section. Send me a photo of your daily planner and I will give you a shout-out all contact details, social links and email at www.roryprendergast.com.

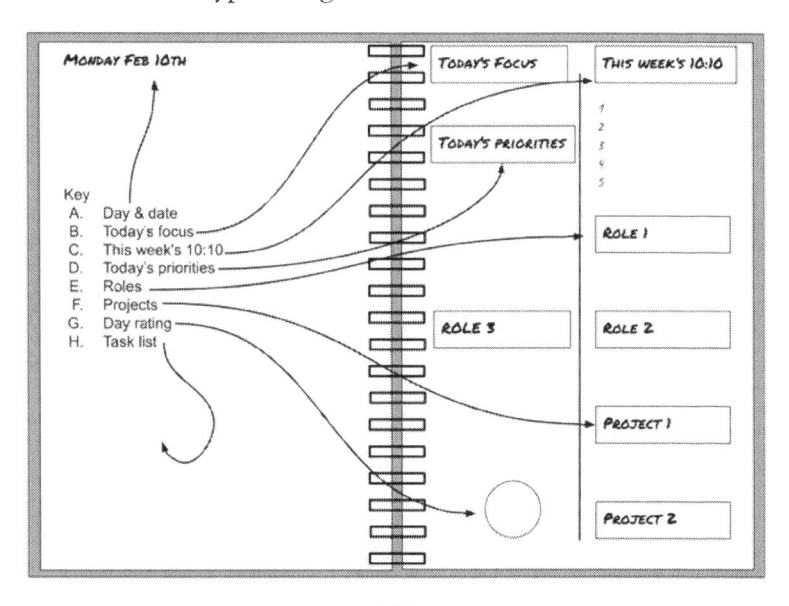

A. Day and date of work, i.e., tomorrow's date
B. Today's focus: the theme for the day
C. This week's 10:10, from your plan for the week
D. Today's priorities: the most important tasks for today
E. Roles, from your vision: what roles have goals today
F. Projects: the tasks for each project or area you are working on
G. Day rating: how did you do today?
H. Task list: list of tasks and activities to be completed today

A. Day and date

If you are writing on Wednesday evening for Thursday, enter Thursday's date here.

B. Today's focus

You will generally leave this section blank until the next day. It comes from your visualization, meditation, or more often the Daily Review in the morning. If nothing comes from any of these, you can choose a focus like "double my income" or something out of your Power Vision – whatever comes to mind naturally that you should focus on. For example: concentrate better after lunch; don't open emails before eleven; pay more attention to co-workers; listen better to your son or daughter.

C. This week's 10:10

The 10-out-of-10 week will form the backbone of your week. It is a shortlist of items that you need to get done this week in order to progress on your goals. This is not your weekly to-do list but a list of top priorities for the week. It should be relatively short, normally three to seven items. On Sunday, take out your monthly plan and determine your 10-out-of-10 week from that plan.

Think about it like this: When you are having a glass of wine on Friday evening, and you look back on the week, what would you need to have checked off to say to yourself, "Well done, that was a 10-out-of-10 week"?

The 10:10 week section on the Daily Planner is carried forward each day, even after items are checked off, by writing them out each day. That way you won't forget anything, and it will drive it further into your subconscious, where the processing occurs.

D. Today's priorities

Of the list of tasks you have today, select one to three that are most important. These are the ones that will help you take small steps towards your vision. There should be no more than one to three priorities for the day. Begin your day with these items, if possible.

E. Roles

The Roles entries will be based on what roles you are working on this month. These come from your Power Vision. Once your planner is written up, identify actions for the roles you are working on. Note them in the Roles section.

F. Projects

You can also include big projects you are working on here. For example, you may be working on your leadership role and have two or three big chunks you want to get out of the way. One of these chunks could also be a project.

G. Day rating

Each evening, rate your day out of 10 so you can review your week and longer-term success.

H. Task list

Now, with your 10-out-of-10 week decided on, what needs to be done tomorrow? On the left hand side is the list of everything you need to do. That includes work, home, self, and relationships. Everything that needs attention during the day goes here: if you've decided to eat vegetarian for the day, to avoid alcohol, or to go to the gym. Everything.

Be animated in this section. Use images, shapes, underlines, whatever feels right. The more feeling you put into this, the better it will work for you. As you complete tasks, cross them off the list with great satisfaction.

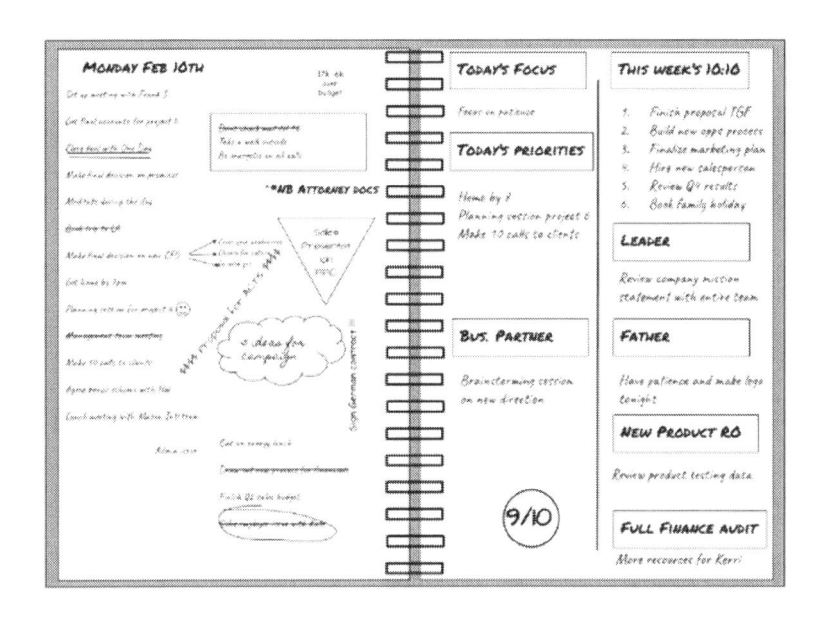

Remember:
- Handwrite everything on paper.
- Draw a line through everything as you complete it.
- Each day, write out the plan for the next day, from start to finish.
- Transcribe your 10:10 week activities across the week to keep track of them (even if done).

The most important thing about the Daily Planner is to write it up the day before. This prepares your subconscious mind, which will be planning and getting ready for the next day.

For years I did a to-do list in the morning, and it can be daunting. It's often a stressful time, and trying to put everything you have to accomplish on a long list before you start makes it look like you have a mountain to climb. Doing it the day before means you start the day more motivated, calm, and effective.

I generally do mine before I leave work, but I start it by 10 AM because stuff crops up during the day – a follow-up, a meeting, etc. – and I need to put it on tomorrow's plan straight away. This means that most of the Daily Planner is written organically throughout the day. I just need to cross the i's, dot the t's, and add a few last items before leaving work.

Writing your to-do list in the evening can help you switch off from work. Maybe you want to make it the very last thing you do before you leave your desk, so you can dedicate your evening to your personal life.

Or maybe you're someone who can't resist bringing a little work home with you, so you put your Planner together after dinner before you finally plop yourself down on the couch. Either way, planning tomorrow's activities serves as the perfect bookend to your workday. Getting all those lingering items out of your head and down on paper makes it much easier to clear your mind, kick back, unwind, and have a great night's sleep.

On our sailing adventure, we visited many ports and harbours. We would stop for the night or sometimes a few days. When the anchor drops after a long voyage, the first thing that comes to mind is a cold beer, but I had a rule on board: No beer until we make a plan for departure the next day. We always planned a day ahead. We would take out the charts and navigation books and plot our route back out to sea, identifying obstacles, currents, and navigational marks. All this was kept in a notebook at the chart table, where it could be grabbed quickly in an emergency.

In certain conditions, *Cerys* and crew were far safer in open sea than at an anchorage. For example, if storm conditions meant that our position became untenable, we may have needed to put to sea quickly, where there are fewer obstacles and therefore less danger, or if we lost our anchor during the night and started drifting. In these situations, we may not have had time to plan our exit. So by creating a plan in the evening, we were fully prepared for such emergencies. Planning for the next day became a habit for us.

This habit has a serious impact on how productive you will be during the day. When you wake up in the morning, you will be completely aware of what needs to be done. Writing the plan down stamps it on your mind from the moment it's written to the time it's crossed off. When you do this, you get more stuff done, and you get more important stuff done.

That's it – your plan is done for tomorrow, and your subconscious is already getting to work. Now you can take a proper rest, relax, and make a break between home and work.

You should not check your email or messages before work in the morning. Enjoy your daily routine, enjoy the time with your family, and enjoy the trip to work – all in the knowledge that you are well prepared for a powerful and productive day.

Once you're at work, the first thing that needs to be opened is your Daily Planner, and the first thing you need to look at is today's priorities. Try to knock one of them out before your coffee and before you open your email.

*

In summary: The Daily Planner is the hub that connects all the elements of the Game Changer Formula. Using this tool will facilitate predictable success. One of the keys is to ensure it is written the day before. That way, your subconscious mind can get to work while your conscious mind can relax and enjoy the evening, free from thoughts of work, deadlines, and challenges.

In the next chapter you will see how to maximize your energy throughout the day by exercising properly.

12. Movement

In this chapter you will explore how movement influences your capacity to achieve predictable success. Movement is an essential component of the Game Changer Formula. It is how you elevate your energy levels so you can perform efficiently and effectively. You must look after your body if you are to achieve the lifetime goals you set for yourself.

Your body is built for movement – not for sitting at a computer screen. Exercise will get the oxygen flowing through your body each morning so you are ready for the day ahead. It will help clear your mind in preparation for a focused and productive day. As the saying goes, "Good things come to those who sweat."

Important: If you have any medical conditions, consult with a physician before you embark on any changes in exercise.

You may think that expending energy will make you more tired and therefore less effective, but the opposite is true. When you exercise in the morning, you feel energy and confidence coursing through you, you can concentrate for longer, and you will sleep better. Exercise can significantly improve your ability to perform productively.

If you are sitting at a desk most of the day, then you are doing exactly the opposite of what you were built for, so you need to compensate with exercise. You should exercise every morning before work if you want to reap the benefits of the Game Changer Formula. Time may be tight, especially if you've got young children in the house. It can be a challenge – but you can find a way to overcome that challenge. You will discover some helpful ideas here.

The reason you need to exercise in the morning, not the evening, as part of the Daily 10, is that your body needs a kickstart in the morning if you are to operate at peak performance. You need to start the flow of oxygen through the brain early, so that when you arrive at work, you feel powerful and ready to take on the day.

> Ship's Log: Dec. 6 – Position 15:30.509N 40:55.803W
>
> Our daily workout lasts 24 hours and covers all major muscle groups, depending on what you are doing. Even sitting is like being on one of those exercise balls, constantly working your abdomen and back muscles to stay in relative synchronization with your surroundings. Hamstrings get a good stretch when working in the galley, as toes are braced against the presses, bum against the companionway, and upper body stretching for the remains of our supplies. Sleep does not arrest this continuous fitness regime – I hold on with my left arm while I sleep, my feet are constantly moving from side to side, and my tongue must also migrate, as I seem to bite it during the night to keep it in place. This does not make for a comfortable breakfast.

I know many people who run or cycle at lunchtime or in the evening for logistical reasons, and that's great, but you will find some routine of movement that you can do in the morning to get yourself pumped up. Even if it's only for five minutes. You will notice the difference in productivity, motivation, and focus with early-morning exercise. If you can get up earlier and do your run or cycle first thing, then that is the ideal solution. If not, find something else you can do in five minutes in the kitchen.

Aerobic or cardio (cardiovascular) exercise is the most important type of exercise you can do. Aerobic exercise is anything that increases the heart rate and gets blood pumping around your system, such as running, brisk walking, or swimming.

Whatever exercise you do should get your heart rate up. The rate will depend on your age, so you should consult a physician on that. I use a heart-rate monitor, but a simple guide is that you should be doing aerobic exercise to a level where it is difficult to hold a conversation. Anything less, and you're not pushing yourself hard enough.

Aerobic exercise improves your cardiovascular health by strengthening your heart and pumping more blood around your system. It lowers blood pressure: a stronger heart can pump more blood with less work, reducing pressure in the arteries. It helps regulate blood sugar, because the muscles use more glucose, reducing the amount in the bloodstream. It can help you sleep: morning exercise induces longer sleep cycles. It boosts brain function. After the age of 30, you begin to lose brain tissue; aerobic exercise can slow that loss and boost cognitive ability. It improves mood and motivation: studies show that even a single session can give you a lift.

A study done at the University of British Columbia found that regular aerobic exercise appears to boost the size of the hippocampus, the area in the brain responsible for memory and learning.

If you don't look after your body, where are you going to live?

As you pass the age of 40, you naturally begin to lose 1 per cent of your muscle mass each year. To combat that, if you're in that age bracket, you should probably be doing some resistance training also. This means working muscles against an external resistance – weights in a gym, resistance bands, or the weight of your own body.

The benefits of resistance training are improved muscle mass and tone, which protect joints and strengthen bones. It builds flexibility and balance, which can help you remain independent as you age. It builds greater stamina: as you get stronger, you won't tire as easily. It improves your posture and mobility. It enhances the performance of everyday tasks and improves self-esteem.

If you are over 40 and intend to live a long and energetic life, you need to begin cardio and resistance training now. Each day that your body wakes up, it makes a call to go into growth mode or decay mode. If you don't challenge it with exercise, it goes into decay mode automatically. You should exercise five days a week, three of them cardio, to keep you alive and growing, and two of them resistance training, to keep your joints and bones in good shape and so you feel like you want to stay alive.

There are other important ways that exercise will help you achieve predictable success.

Regular physical activity affects energy production at a cellular level, giving a boost to the cell's powerhouses in the brain and helping it to work more efficiently. This will help you with focus, innovation, motivation, and creativity.

Even short bursts of activity can help to keep your mind clear and alert. By increasing blood flow to the brain, you sharpen your awareness and will more readily identify opportunities for growth.

Exercise stimulates the pituitary gland to release endorphins. These trigger a euphoric feeling that can help with motivation – not just during the exercise but also in the workplace after a session. Exercise stimulates the generation of new neurons and protects existing neurons, helping to develop your sense of clarity.

You have been given your body, and you should make the most of it. Think of it as an instrument that requires some fine-tuning. As a kid, I didn't do a lot of exercise, and it wasn't until 2006 that I began to take it seriously at all. I was challenged by a friend to run the Connemara half-marathon in the west of Ireland. So I bought running shoes and had a go. At first I wasn't able to run a hundred yards, but bit by bit I improved, and I just kept at it, a couple of times a week, until I started to enjoy it.

Today my routine is a 5-kilometre (3-mile) run at six thirty AM from my house to the diving board in Salthill, Galway. I jump into the sea in my shorts and then run back home to dry off.

These mornings it's dark from start to finish, and the water is 8–9 degrees Celsius (about 46 Fahrenheit). It's a refreshing start to the day, to say the least. I have come to love the dark cold water shock in the mornings.

Two days a week, I replace that with a gym session that involves resistance training and core exercises. I take Saturday off, and on Sunday I do an hour of yoga with my yoga teacher Dave Cunningham of the Yoga Shala. Dave runs a tough practice, and it's the hardest exercise session of the week.

Running is great exercise once you know how to do it properly. I have trained with an Irish ex-Olympian in running technique, specifically to avoid running stress and injury. We have even developed a beta version of an online training programme together. If it's up and running when you read this, you can access it here www.roryprendergast.com/bookresources.

My exercise routine takes me about 45 minutes each morning when I include all the warming up, cooling down, and stretches for my back. So it's quite a commitment. I do it because I love it and because I am working on what I call the Epic Project, which is a venture to live to 120+ years and enjoy every minute of it. I want to bring other people along on the journey, but we will talk about that later.

You do not need to run 5 km a day or spend 45 minutes exercising to implement the Game Changer Formula. But if you want to have predictable success, you absolutely need to incorporate at least 5–10 minutes of movement into your morning.

Exercise doesn't have to be hard or complicated, You can do something at home in your kitchen. I will share some ideas for 5–10 minute routines, but you can easily find or create your own. It should be fun, not a chore, so find something that suits you and that you will miss if you can't make it.

Running works for me, because I don't need equipment and it's a great way to see a new city early in the morning when I'm travelling. I've noticed that the earlier I go out for a run, and the worse the weather, the friendlier the other runners. I love cold wet days because I meet determined people.

I run to clear my mind. I run for my daily energy. I need my exercise so that I feel powerful and focused when I arrive at my desk. Some kind of enthusiasm switch gets flicked on at around the 4 km mark that drives me for the rest of the day.

Find what ticks the boxes for you, whether it's yoga, core workout, Pilates, or spinning. There's a YouTube video just a click away to help you through it. Get ready the night before. I leave my running gear in the hall outside my bedroom so I don't wake my wife. I dress in the dark there so I don't wake my son. It means that sometimes my shorts are on backwards or my T-shirt is inside out!

Now, at 50, I am fitter, faster, and stronger – both mentally and physically – than I have ever been in my life.

*

In summary: Movement is one of the steps that engages the energy component of the Game Changer Formula. Exercise empowers the body and mind to support your quest for the life you deserve. You cannot achieve that without a fit, fast, and flexible mind and body. Exercise brings many benefits that you may not have been aware of. One of them is fun: exercise should always be fun. Find the exercise that brings out the fun and the success in you. You'll find exercise ideas in Chapter 25.

When you exercise, pay particular attention to hydration. In the next chapter you will discover how water is critically important to ensure that your body and brain are functioning efficiently, which is vital to achieving predictable success.

13. Hydration

Hydration is one of the simplest things you can work on to help you achieve your vision. Water can have a major impact on your energy levels, brain function, and physical performance. In this chapter you will learn why it is so important and how to ensure you stay hydrated for maximum results.

> *Water is the driving force of all nature.* —Leonardo da Vinci

I never really thought much about water. When Ursula and I needed to learn how to survive in a life raft for an extended period, we took a course on survival at sea. Something that struck me deeply on that course was that we would be able to live for three minutes without air, three days without water, and three weeks without food. I don't ever want to prove any of those assertions. Only three days without water. It may seem obvious, but I hadn't realized how important water was.

Water became a critical resource in my sailing plan. We needed to either carry enough water for four people for five weeks, or install a water maker that would turn seawater into drinking water through reverse osmosis. It uses a lot of electrical power – another scarce resource on a sailing yacht. I decided we could do without washing ourselves for the passage, and that we could cook with salt water. We stocked up on baby wipes to keep ourselves semi-hygienic. I was grateful for a shower at the end of the trip.

Ship's Log: Dec. 12 – Position 14:35.361N 55:45.434W

We have just come through a 40-knot squall and reached speeds of 9.4 knots. We had slowed down to about 7.5 knots when a wave stopped us dead in the water. It was like a removal van jamming on the brakes to avoid hitting a kid. Everything flew out of cupboards and shelves, and the noise, although not hugely loud, was unbearable. You imagine all the damage that is being done as loose crockery, equipment, and food take the opportunity to test their gravitational pull. Tom was pelted by lemons again in his stock of a bunk.

Things back in their place, I am on watch and the swell is heavy. It is rhythmic enough to be just about bearable apart from when we get a wave just under the quarter. This attempts to spin *Cerys* around 180 degrees, and she shudders and vibrates as she battles these dragons, always conquering; she is our knight in white armour, our slayer of beasts. The main sheet has gone slack. A sudden wind shift of 90 degrees to the south catches me off guard at 4 AM, and I rip off my iPod, as it can get tangled in the wheel and I need to be able to hear what's happening with the sails in the dark. Putting her on a northerly course asap to prevent the gybe, Debbie Harry is still belting it out. I am confused. As the compass comes round to 350, I can see what I have done. In the rush I had undone my harness, my lifeline, instead of the iPod, and I feel kind of naked up here on my own without it. At night and in this sea, if I go overboard, I'm finished, and nobody would know for another two hours. There is no chance of rescue.

Beastly encounters were common today. In the morning we were approached to starboard by another, this time mammalian rather than reptilian, *Balaenoptera acutorstrata*, a minke whale. All 10 metres of her coasted up alongside, and she flipped first on her side and then on her back, remaining abeam of us and studying *Cerys*'s hull and possibly us. Then, with one flick of the tail, she disappeared beneath us forward of our keel and out on our port side.

Our kitchen knives have rusted, we have torn our mainsail cover, and I am being very wary of our port, and last, water tank. The gauge is showing full for the last week, and I know this cannot be correct. This is the thing that makes me most nervous. We must maintain reserves of water. We can survive only 3 days without it.

A survey of over 3,000 Americans found that three quarters of them probably suffered net fluid loss during the day, resulting in chronic dehydration. It found that while Americans drank about eight servings of hydrating drinks per day, this was offset by caffeinated beverages, alcohol, and a high-salt diet.

Water is needed for digestion and for absorption of vitamins and nutrients. It detoxifies the liver and kidneys and carries waste away. But most people don't know that water is critically important for brain function. Your brain is about three-quarters water and is strongly influenced by hydration status. Water is essential for distributing nutrients to the brain and for removing toxins. When your brain is fully hydrated, these processes are more efficient, improving concentration and mental alertness.

Studies show that even mild dehydration (1–3% of body weight) can impair many aspects of brain function. When you are properly hydrated, you think faster, remain focused for longer, and experience greater clarity and creativity. This can have a massive impact on your capacity to achieve your desired outcome.

Most people don't know that water is critically important for brain function.

A study among young women found that fluid loss of just 1.36% after exercise impaired mood and concentration and increased the frequency of headaches. A study among young men showed that fluid loss of 1.59% was detrimental to working memory and increased anxiety and fatigue.

A 1–3% loss of fluid is about 1.5–4.5 pounds (0.5–2 kg) of body weight for a 150-pound (68 kg) person. This can easily happen through normal activity. If you are exercising or spend time in warm or air-conditioned environments, that loss can be substantially more. Dehydration can make you more tired, lower your motivation, and lead to a change in body-temperature control. It can make exercise feel more difficult, both physically and mentally. That is not surprising when you consider that muscle is 80% water.

Dehydration has been shown in some studies to trigger headaches or migraines. Hydration has been shown to alleviate certain types of headaches in some people. Optimal hydration can prevent these adverse effects and may even reduce the oxidative stress that occurs during high-intensity exercise.

Water can also be helpful for weight loss. It can alleviate the feeling of hunger and can increase your metabolic rate. One study asked people to drink half a litre of water (17 ounces), and their metabolic rate increased by 24–30% for up to an hour and a half. Timing can also have an impact. People who drank half a litre of water before meals lost 44% more weight over 12 weeks than those who did not. From a weight-loss point of view, water is best drunk cold, as it uses more calories to bring it up to body temperature.

Important: If you have any medical condition, you should check with your doctor, as it is possible to drink too much water with certain medical conditions.

If you want to achieve your Power Vision, you need to function at optimum levels both mentally and physically. Therefore you need to understand and manage hydration. So how much water should you drink? The National Academies of Sciences, Engineering, and Medicine determined that an adequate daily fluid intake is about 15.5 cups (3.7 litres) for men and about 11.5 cups (2.7 litres) for women.

If you are someone who doesn't drink enough water during the day, you may find it difficult to reach optimal hydration straight away. Take it step by step. Here are some useful tips:

- If you're thirsty, you're already dehydrated – don't allow yourself become thirsty.
- Take it slowly – you don't need to go from zero to 3.7 litres in a day.

- Use a phone or watch app to measure your intake.
- Focus on progress rather than the end goal.
- Get a measured water bottle for your desk, and keep it in sight all the time.
- If you don't like the taste, add some lemon.
- Avoid sweetened flavourings.
- Eat foods with a high water content (cucumbers and tomatoes are 95% water).
- Avoid foods with high salt content.
- Set a reminder on your phone or watch to drink water every 30 minutes.
- A quick urine check is the best do-it-yourself way to ensure you are hydrated: anything darker than pale yellow means you need to hydrate.

*

In summary: Much of your body is water: 75% of your brain, 80% of your muscle, and 82% of your blood. Dehydration has a major impact on both mental and physical performance. Understand and manage your hydration to perform at a level that will produce predictable success. If you are thirsty, you are already dehydrated. Motivate, hydrate, feel great!

In the next chapter, you will discover how fuelling your body correctly throughout the day can enhance your performance, and how acquiring a better understanding of what you eat can help you live a longer and more prosperous life.

14. Fuel

To achieve continuous success, you will need energy. To generate energy, you'll need to burn fuel. The fuel you burn is food. It is important to understand how best to fuel your mind and body to achieve the life you deserve. If you are burning the incorrect mix of fuel for your body, your energy will deplete and you will not have the power to achieve predictable success. This chapter is about correct fuelling.

> *Those who have no time for healthy eating will sooner or later have to find time for illness.* —Edward Stanley

Most of the Daily 10s in this book are new things you need to start doing. This one, fuelling, is one that you are already doing. You just need to ensure you are doing it in a way that is in harmony with the other nine.

You are what you eat – literally. Your body is made up of the food you eat plus a few other things you draw from the environment, like oxygen, vitamin D, and bacteria. If you are what you eat, and your food is the fuel that will supply the energy needed to reach your goals, shouldn't you put some thought into it?

We are all different. Your ideal fuel mix depends on your genes, your level of activity, what you currently eat, and how your body works. I believe each of us should seek professional guidance on nutrition. Learn what foods support you in fulfilling your goals, and what foods limit your potential. Do this by identifying the best dietician or nutritionist in your area and making an appointment. Look for someone who specializes in nutrition and diet only. (Many nutritionists offer multiple other services, like reflexology and fertility, or promote a specific food regime.)

I am not qualified to advise on nutrition. I have neither training nor experience in it. You should consult a nutrition expert or physician before changing your diet. What I can do is share my beliefs about food and describe how I use food as fuel for energy, which increases my productivity and supports an active and healthy life.

What I cover here is what I have learned works for my body over many years, along with expert advice I have received from my dietician. When I talk about health, I mean both physical and mental health; when I talk about energy, I mean both physical and brain power. Your brain weighs only about three pounds but uses about a quarter of your food, energy, and oxygen to operate, so it's an important part of the equation.

> Ship's Log: May 14 – Position 32:51N 47:59W – Wind W Force 5, Heavy Swell, Rain, and Squalls
>
> The bananas have fully ripened, many beyond ripeness. Black and soft, they are still tasty if sucked through a small hole in the bottom. The avocados and custard apples

finished, we still have plenty of apples, oranges, melons, cucumbers, and a few very ripe tomatoes. The only thing we have run out of is cereal. We still have our fresh bread daily and plenty of milk, water, etc. We are quite happy with our provisioning. Our power management has been successful up to now. We are careful with plotter screens, lighting, and pumps. Our LED nav lights and solar-powered LED cabin lights have made a huge saving in amp hour terms, and we have managed to keep the batteries above 80% almost all the time. Plenty of diesel left also.

In the galley the competition is heating up. Gordon Ramsay versus Jamie Oliver versus all of Sicily. Sicily was on top in the bread wars and has definitely won the battered kitchen award. Flanno makes a meal like a hit man in a butcher shop. Joey picks up the pieces.

Competition update: Joey thinks he's ahead on the bread. Big is not necessarily beautiful, Joe. I am in the lead in the bread wars. The eggs were rotten today, and the bananas didn't survive the squall.

PS: The bread wars took an unexpected turn as Flanno extracted a golden crust from the oven. Oddly, my hard-earned muesli disappeared at the same time. Crust broken, mystery solved. Behold my sacred muesli in Flanno's loaf! The foulest expletives accompanied the de-heeling of this oaty creation, and Flanno was forced under maritime law to a credit me with 20% of the success.

Another morning battle draws closed, my mind encrusted with strategies for tomorrow's struggle. Kneading a plan, this yeast will rise again in triumph.

There is a tendency to associate eating properly with weight loss. It seems that when you speak about food and exercise, people assume you are talking about losing weight. It is not the same thing. Weight loss may be something you want to work on – diet and exercise certainly affect that – but there are other important reasons for eating well and exercising. So break that mental link between those two elements before reading on.

It is important to enjoy food. I do. Food is a tool we can use to optimize health, but it is a source of pleasure too. Pleasure is important for optimizing mental and physical health. So it is important not to restrict your diet to the point where pleasure is diminished. I only want to live to 120-plus if I can enjoy it, and food is an integral part of enjoying my life.

You are what you eat – literally.

I want to eat food that is good for me and good for my environment. I believe in reducing the toxins I ingest and increasing the food that promotes health. I believe in balancing my food intake with my activity levels. This should be achieved with practical application and with moderation.

It seems that when something is identified as good for you, it must form 30 per cent of your diet. If something is identified as unhealthy, it must be eliminated from your diet. The result is an unbalanced approach to nutrition: Don't eat carbs, eliminate red meat, reduce fat, eat full fat, plant-based is the only way, fast intermittently, get rid of gluten, avoid dairy, get on the keto diet, etc. The truth lies in balance, moderation, and understanding how your body works.

I generally resist what I perceive as extreme food regimes. I believe most weight-loss diets are unsustainable over the long term, and I don't feel that we all need to live on a plant-based diet to save ourselves and the planet. It has become almost impossible to research anything on nutrition online. Almost every article seems to have some bias, most of what you read is contradicted in the next article, and very few authors speak of balance and moderation.

When I eat badly, my performance drops. When I eat well, my capacity to produce predictable success increases. By and large we eat poorly today, and I see three root causes:

- Choice
- Education
- Time.

Choice

It can be difficult to find good food. As I write this, in Santiago, it has taken me quite a bit of effort to discover places where I can buy non-processed food. In the average supermarket you are deluded into believing you have infinite choice, but in reality most of the food on the shelves is of one kind: highly processed, and built for long shelf life, not nutrition. It's hard to determine what's actually in the packet.

At home in Galway, Ireland, here's how we choose better. Every Saturday, my son and I visit the local market. We are lucky to have this centuries-old market, which takes place just outside St. Nicholas's Church, which was founded in 1320. We taste new foods and buy as much colourful and fun food as we can. I look at this as buying energy for myself and the family. I try to stick with foods that are local and close to the farm. I buy organic meat, organic fruit and vegetables, and wild fish.

I have learned to love different leafy vegetables and fruits. That wasn't easy for me. Part of eating healthy food is finding new ways to enjoy it. At times I have had to put in a little effort to get to like something. It is important to me to understand what goes into my body and to teach my son about food. Easier said than done, but he is well known at the fish stall and the cheese stall. I also started planting vegetables on our balcony, so even though we live in the city, we grow varieties of lettuce, herbs, and a few vegetables. By putting in some fun time on Saturday, we make it easier to make great food choices for the rest of the week.

The same principle applies to my work area. I ensure I have a good supply of nuts and non-sugary snacks in my drawer, so that when I need something quick there are good choices to hand. If I didn't have that, I would be running to the nearest store, where my choice would be limited.

I also bring my own lunch to work every day, which normally consists of 90 per cent mixed and spicy salad leaves, with smoked fish or another source of protein. I keep a bottle of olive oil at my desk and put a quarter lemon in my lunchbox: that solves the salad dressing issue, which can be tricky at work. Again, that good choice is made in plenty of time on Saturday when buying for the week, not last-minute when you're starving at lunchtime in the office.

Do we eat frozen pizza? Sometimes. Things don't always go according to plan, and that's okay. You need to be practical too. Most of what I eat is good, nutrient-rich food, and the weekly diet is balanced with proteins, fats, and carbohydrates.

Education

Most of us don't really understand food, which is amazing when you think about it. There are two areas: understanding how important food is, which we have just discussed, and understanding how to ensure you can fit a healthy diet into your current lifestyle.

We have become removed from food production. Surveys in the UK and Australia show that many children have no idea where a lot of food comes from: they think strawberries grow in the fridge, they believe milk comes from a supermarket, and they have no clue that broccoli is a plant. If they don't understand the basics, then how will they ever understand food labelling, which seems designed to bewilder? How will they learn to make great choices in food? And if they can't make great food choices, how will that affect who they become, and what their ultimate potential is?

Both children and adults need to learn more about food so that we can make more informed decisions on something that can have a dramatic impact on our quality of life. I have been lucky: my generation in Ireland was never that far from where food is grown or produced. I spent my summers on my uncle's farm, and my mother has a passion for food. We were never given candy, sweets, or soft drinks when I was a kid. That has had a big impact on me – I don't recall buying a packet of sweets in the last 20 years.

That passion for food trickled down from my mother to me and all my siblings. I worked as a chef and ran a hotel, my sister is a food writer and photographer, and my brother feeds thousands of people a day in his catering business. So I have had a head start. But my food philosophy is simple, and anyone can adopt it.

Time

Most of us are time poor because we have so much going on in our crazy lives. So we outsource dinner time to a factory. If you don't have time to cook in the evening, the easiest thing to do is buy a frozen pizza. My son and I have changed food shopping from a chore into a fun learning experience. When we visit the market, we are spending quality time together and learning about nutrition, energy, and food. This is one way we overcome the time issue – simply by changing the mindset from chore to fun time.

My son generally selects the fish from the fishmonger. The deal is "He who chooses prepares", so he learns from the fishmonger how to prepare that particular fish, including cleaning it and removing guts or scales. He has been known to get a friend involved when confronted with squid tentacles.

When we come home, we cook. On Saturday evening, we batch-cook dinners, school lunches, and work lunches and freeze what we can. The freezer is our friend. This is another way we save time during the week. There is always something at hand, pre-portioned either for an individual or for the family, and it takes no time to get meals ready Monday to Friday when we are all busy.

My plan is not fool-proof:

Fruit

I was never a big fruit eater. I try my best to get some into my body each day by turning them into smoothies and drinks. This means it's a little more fun and more likely to work for me. I chop fruits and vegetables and freeze them so I always have a variety. I keep frozen ginger too, so the morning juices are always interesting. I use whatever fresh fruit I have and add frozen carrot chunks, cucumber, and grated ginger. It tastes great. I know it's not the ideal way to consume fruit, as some of the nutrients are knocked out, but it's better than not eating fruit at all in the short term while I get better at liking it.

Supermarket

We still end up in the supermarket sometimes. When I'm there I make the best choices I can. I try to stick to foods that have fewer than five ingredients. I avoid anything that has "low" or "zero" on it, because I know that when food processing companies take an ingredient out, they add something else to make it taste good. So if they remove fat, they add things like sugars and hydrogenated fats.

Hydrogenated fats are liquid fats that have been chemically altered to change their melting point so they can be solid at room temperature. They provide a specific consistency to a processed food. They make it "spreadable" so you can use it on your toast, for example. When unsaturated fats are hydrogenated, they form trans fats. Trans fats appear naturally in animal products, and moderate intake of these natural trans fats is not considered to be harmful. Artificial trans fats, however, are thought to raise "bad" cholesterol and lower "good" cholesterol, contributing to heart disease.

In diet and low-sugar products, manufacturers replace sugar with compounds like aspartame, which has been claimed to cause problems from headaches to cancer, although food safety authorities generally consider it safe. I just don't like the sound of it.

Alcohol

Where alcohol is concerned, I definitely need to make some improvements. But it's not something I want to eliminate completely, as I enjoy beer and wine. The current recommended intake is a maximum of 14 units per week, but that can be difficult to understand. Units vary greatly: beers can differ in strength from 2.5 to 8 per cent or more.

With the help of my local bar owner, Conor, I have devised a weekly plan to keep me at 14 units. I did a beer tasting to compare the beers I like and their different strengths. I found one that I like that is relatively low in alcohol. Conor ensures that every time I order a beer, he brings me a half pint, not a pint as would be customary in Ireland. Each is 0.85 of a unit. I also identified a wine I like at the lower end of the alcohol spectrum. This means I can have seven beers a week and one bottle of wine and remain within the 14 units. Barely.

You can work out how many units there are in any drink by multiplying its strength or ABV (as a percentage) by its volume (in millilitres) and dividing the result by 1,000. For example, for a pint (568 ml) of strong lager (5.2%), it's 5.2 × 568 ÷ 1,000 = 2.95 units. Five pints of lager would put you over the weekly limit.

Sometimes, of course, things don't go according to plan – I have a few friends who can push me off target!

One last thing on alcohol. Your liver prioritizes it, so if it's working on alcohol every day, it may miss out on some other functions. Try to keep at least two or three days during the week completely alcohol free to give your liver a chance to get through its workload.

*

In summary: Think of food as the fuel that delivers the energy for your success. You need to take the correct fuel on board for you. This is so important that I suggest you take professional advice from a dietician. Food should be enjoyed: whether you're cooking it, buying it, or eating it, make it a positive experience for you and the next generation.

In the next chapter you will discover how important sleep is to everything. You will learn how sleep can affect your ability to perform, and what you can change to ensure that your sleep is facilitating predictable success.

15. The Early 8

The Early 8 is all about sleep and recovery. This is part of the energy component in the Game Changer Formula. If you don't get your sleep right, then everything falls apart. From today on, sleep must be a priority for you.

Lack of sleep and poor-quality sleep affect your physical health and mental capacity. You will not achieve your potential without proper sleep. The Early 8 means that as part of the Daily 10, you need to get to bed early, get eight hours of good-quality sleep, and get up early.

> *Early to bed and early to rise makes a man healthy, wealthy, and wise.* —Traditional proverb

Before my son was born, I was anxious about sleep. I had heard many parents speak about sleep deprivation when a newborn baby arrives. My wife would be shattered after childbirth, and I need my sleep.

I knew that solo long-distance sailors sleep in short naps – 20 minutes at a time, night and day – so they can keep watch. I studied how this worked and trained myself to do it so I could function on less sleep. The first night we brought my son home, he slept all night and continued to do so. I guess he needed his sleep as much as I did. I think I could have managed the naps for a short period, but I am now sure it would have been bad for my health.

If you want to live a life of significance and reach your goals, you need to prioritize sleep.

Sleep has a critical impact on our physical and mental health. It gives us the recovery time our body and mind need after a hard day. Think of it like aircraft maintenance. Every aircraft has a maintenance schedule depending on hours flown, take-offs, landings, and make and model. Most aircraft get 12 hours' maintenance a week to keep them flying. This prevents things from going wrong. If an aircraft doesn't get enough maintenance hours, then some servicing will not get done. That will eventually cause a problem.

Likewise, your body and mind need scheduled maintenance in the form of sleep every day. You can skimp for a while, but something will break. For your health and productivity, you need to prioritize sleep. If you don't get enough maintenance hours, then some of the jobs just don't get done. Something will break down.

Onboard *Cerys*, we divided our watches into three-hour shifts. One crew member would take watch to ensure the safety of the crew and vessel while the others rested. Resting was obligatory. Your duty was to prioritize sleep. You were responsible for the lives of your crew mates while they slept, so it was important that you were well rested in order to remain vigilant while on duty.

> Ship's Log: May 13 – Position 32:51N 50:00W – Wind SE Force 5, 1,096 nautical miles to Horta, Full Sail, 5.3 knots, 062 degrees True
>
> I saw a large turtle yesterday, but the unfortunate animal was attached to a piece of timber about the same size as its body by a length of fishing net. Under calmer circumstances I would have stopped, but we have a big 4–5 metre swell running from the north west at the moment.
>
> One man down tonight, minor illness. We can easily cover the shifts for a day or two if necessary, but it really confirms the fact that we need a team of four aboard for a trip like this. It's like missing a link. The team is working extremely well. It's good to feel you can sleep confidently at night with trust in whoever is on watch.

Here are some of the things that happen while you sleep.

Data processing

Your brain doesn't shut down when you sleep. In fact, it's quite busy, taking all the information you gathered throughout the day, sorting it out, and filing it away in the right places. This is important for long-term memory. Sleep improves memory.

Repair

While you sleep, your body is flooded with hormones that work on different parts of your body and brain. One of these is melatonin, whose job is to regulate your sleep pattern. Other hormones are secreted for growth and repair, which maintain your body overnight. Getting insufficient or poor-quality sleep can hinder that repair.

Relaxing

When you sleep, your sympathetic nervous system gets a chance to unwind. This is the controller for your "fight or flight" response. If it does not get a chance to rest, it increases in activity, leading to an increase in blood pressure.

Fighting

During sleep, your immune system releases proteins called cytokines. Their job is to fight inflammation, infection, and trauma. If you are not getting enough sleep, your immune system is not functioning optimally.

Waste disposal

During sleep, the brain turns on the glymphatic system, which acts like a sewer, helping to clear out the waste that brain cells generate during regular tasks. The brain has a finite amount of energy at its disposal. It must choose between two different states: awake and aware, or asleep and repair. It cannot do both simultaneously.

Most people need only three to four hours of sleep a night to maintain minimal cognitive brain function – the processes responsible for carrying out everyday things like driving a car or getting dressed. So you can *survive* on less sleep for a period. However, if you need to focus and concentrate, for example on problem solving, your brain appears to need eight hours' sleep for that kind of task.

Different age groups need different amounts of sleep. The US National Sleep Foundation recommends the following:

Age	Hours of sleep
Older adults 65+	7–8
Adults 26–64	7–9
Young adults 18–25	7–9
Teenagers 14–17	8–10
School-age children 6–13	9–11
Preschool children 3–5	10–13
Toddlers 1–2	11–14
Infants 4–11 months	12–15
Newborns 0–3 months	14–17

Adequate sleep is not just about the number of hours: there is also quality to consider. Many factors can undermine the quality of your sleep, and you should be aware of them and reduce their impact as much as possible.

Alcohol

As many as 20 per cent of Americans use alcohol to help them fall asleep. Alcohol is a depressant and can induce drowsiness, helping you fall asleep. But it has a negative impact on the quality of sleep.

Having more than one or two drinks shortly before bedtime causes increased awakenings due to alcohol's arousal effect as it is metabolized during the night. You should avoid alcohol a couple of hours before bedtime to get the best-quality sleep.

Caffeine

Caffeine is the world's most widely used stimulant. It keeps you awake by not allowing cells to sense adenosine, a chemical that builds up in the brain to cause sleepiness. Even if caffeine does not stop you falling asleep, it affects the quality of your sleep by changing the sleep pattern and causing more awakenings, which you may not even remember.

Even if you think caffeine doesn't affect your sleep, it probably does. Caffeine has a quarter life of 12 hours, which means that if you drink a cup at midday, one quarter of its caffeine is still in your system at midnight. Try to drink it only in the morning.

Light

Light affects sleep directly by making it harder to fall asleep, and indirectly by affecting your circadian rhythms – your internal clock – which tell you when it's time for sleep. That clock is influenced by light-sensitive cells in your retina. It naturally knows when to fall asleep. But since the invention of electric light, sleep time has tended to be pushed later.

Even worse, the blue light emitted by phones and TVs screens is much closer to sunlight than incandescent light is. Screen light has a substantial impact on your internal clock, and our exposure to it affects sleep quality and makes us want to sleep later.

To minimize the effect of artificial light on sleep, you should do a few things. Turn down lights in the house around two hours before bedtime. Do this with dimmer switches or by turning off brighter lights. Ensure that your sleep environment is as dark as possible – even bright clocks and LEDs can impact your sleep.

Eliminate screens two hours before bedtime, or at least use a setting or an app, like f.lux, that changes your screen light with the time of day. Use blackout blinds in your bedroom, or wear a sleep mask.

Temperature

Sleep in a cool room, about 15–18°C or 60–67°F. Your body temperature decreases by one to two degrees to initiate sleep, and a cooler room facilitates this. It will help you fall asleep more quickly and get better-quality sleep during the night.

Stress

People who experience stress, anxiety, and depression usually find it harder to fall asleep and tend to sleep lightly. They generally have more REM sleep and less deep sleep. This is probably because their bodies are programmed to respond to stressful and potentially dangerous situations by waking up. Stress, even that caused by daily concerns, can stimulate this arousal response and make restful sleep harder to achieve. To combat this, seek advice on stress or use meditation and exercise to relieve it.

Busy mind

When you have a busy day, you are bombarded from all sides with messages, demands, and tasks. It's only when you put your head on the pillow that you have the time and capacity to run through the day. Only then do you remember things you should have done, which causes stress and impacts falling asleep and sleep quality.

Keep a notebook beside your bed. Then, if those thoughts come to you, export them to the notebook. Keep your mind clear and ready for a great night's sleep. You can also rely on your Daily Review to pick up anything important that you may have missed.

Timing

Sleep times should be consistent. Without a routine, it can be difficult to fall asleep. Create a fairly strict sleep routine. Go to bed at the same time, and get up at the same time. Keep your bedroom for sleeping, so your mind knows what to expect when you go there. If it's a place for TV or gaming, then your mind doesn't know what to expect when you enter the bedroom.

Don't let your subconscious think that your bed is a place to stay awake in. If you can't sleep in 15–20 minutes, get out of bed, read a book until you feel sleepy, then go back to bed.

A major study on sleep duration among 150,000 adults working in different occupations found that the prevalence of inadequate sleep – defined as seven hours or less – increased from 31% in 2010 to 36% in 2018. People are getting less sleep for many reasons.

If you want to live a life of significance and reach your goals, you need to prioritize sleep. Set a time for going to bed and a time for waking up, and stick to them. You may find that you need to get up earlier than before to get your routine done each day, and this may be difficult for a while until your body gets used to it. But if you are getting enough good-quality sleep, then it will not be a problem in the long term.

If you are someone who uses the snooze button, here is something you can do to stop that habit. As soon as your alarm goes off, count backwards from five: "5, 4, 3, 2, 1…", then jump straight out. I can't remember the last time I used a snooze button, and I was a heavy user.

*

In summary: Sleep is what repairs your body and your mind and sets you up for action the next day. Without it, you cannot implement the Game Changer Formula. You need to prioritize sleep quantity and quality and get eight great hours every night. Get to bed early and get up early.

In Part 3 of the book, you will learn how to get started with the Daily 10 and how to deal with challenges.

Part 3: Getting Started

16. Let's Get Moving

You are already more than good enough to achieve what you want out of life. In this chapter you will learn how to pull all the parts together into a simple daily routine to achieve predictable success. You will see how to implement the Daily 10. It's easy. If I can do it, anyone can – but you'll need to take action.

> *An idea not coupled with action will never get any bigger than the brain cell it occupied.* —Arnold Glasow

The past is done. It's fixed. The future can be similar, or it can be different. As you learn to train your subconscious, change your habits, and direct your imagination, you will improve your life consciously, in its entirety. But you need to decide now. Are you going to live the life you deserve, or merely exist?

If you choose to live the life you deserve, then you need to develop habits of success. Habits are just things you do that you don't even think about. That is how the Daily 10 will feel in time.

In Chapter 5, I touched on the fact that I learned more from transatlantic sailing than from any study or course. A lot of the Game Changer Formula and Daily 10 come from that experience.

On a transatlantic voyage, you need to cover sea miles every day. Our goal was a hundred nautical miles a day, most of them hopefully in the right direction. The boat never stops. You sail day and night. Every wave tries to push you off course, but you have complete clarity on the target and you keep pointing the bow back at your destination.

Storms will force you to alter course and lose ground. You will steer back on course as soon as it's safe. Equipment will break, but you'll fix it and keep going to ensure you are covering a hundred miles a day. That voyage was a massive achievement for my wife and me, especially because of our lack of sailing experience.

Ship's Log: Arc Start

Today is the day. Very nervous this morning – 218 boats leaving the marina at the same time is a little unnerving. Luckily I have had good manoeuvring practice queuing for the fuel dock. Nice NE breeze at the line, which is between a Navy ship and the west shore of Las Palmas. Too many boats for me to manage the start, so I have handed the helm to Jeannot.

We were in the first 10 boats across the line and in the thick of it. Adrenaline high and pumped higher by Ursula's screams. We were pushed up and managed to squeeze through. Unfortunately we had a better start than the big boats, so as they overtook us we lost the wind for about 3 minutes. Glad to be out the other side and still in the head of the pack, nice to look back on the others, but we will take it easy now. As spinnakers fly, flap, and twist around forestays we are settling down and headed south towards the Cape Verdes, where we will turn west when we pick up the trades.

As night falls, the fleet has scattered and we are doing up to 8 knots. One racing boat has covered 60 miles in 4 hours.

To achieve the life you deserve, you too need to progress every day in the right direction. The Daily 10 ensures you succeed at that. But if you leave out any parts, it becomes less effective.

One important thing I have learned from sailing is balance. On a boat, ten components work together to get you safely to your destination, and there is a balance between them. The forces work together to achieve the desired outcome. No one thing works without its balancing equivalent.

Balancing components of a sailing yacht

Sails	↔	Hull
Keel	↔	Mast
Rudder	↔	Wheel
Boom	↔	Sheets (ropes used to control a sail)
Crew	↔	Navigation system

If you remove any component, you get washed ashore somewhere of nature's choosing, not of yours, and that's if you're lucky. The Daily 10 works exactly the same way: If you leave out one component, you can end up somewhere you never wanted to be. But I guarantee that if you apply the Game Changer Formula in full by implementing the Daily 10, it will improve your life.

How does the Daily 10 ensure that the Game Changer Formula is executed? Let's look at the formula and how the Daily 10 relates to it and the steps you'll need to go through.

The Game Changer Formula

$$(\text{Mindset} + \text{Energy} + \text{Accountability})^{\text{Vision}} = \text{Predictable Success}$$

The table below shows how each activity in the Daily 10 achieves at least one component in the Game Changer Formula. You don't need to remember the formula, but you do need to write and implement the Daily 10. In full. Every day.

Game Changer Formula + Daily 10	Mindset	Energy	Accountability	Vision
Mindset Manual	✓			
Stillness	✓			
Imagination	✓			✓
Daily Review	✓		✓	
Movement	✓	✓		
Fuel		✓		
Hydration		✓		
Daily Planner			✓	✓
Check-in	✓		✓	
Early 8		✓		

You may be telling yourself that this is all too much. I can understand that. Successful people make decisions quickly and change them slowly. Make a fast decision right now to do this, and in return I will show you a step-by-step path to turning this into a habit, something you will not even think about.

When I started this, I began with all the Daily 10 on the first day. That won't suit everybody. Most of the people I have worked with on this needed a little time to get to that point. I have developed a step-by-step guide for 12 days over three weeks to get you where you need to be. If you're the kind of person who goes all in, great. Do it. If you want to take it step by step, follow the process below.

If you choose to live the life you deserve, then you will need to develop habits of success.

The Daily 10 is intended for use Monday to Friday. It's good to get a break on the weekend. This plan is for Monday to Friday over three weeks, with twelve days of Daily 10s over that period. If tomorrow is Thursday, don't wait for Monday. Get started straight away.

Evening zero

Reread Chapter 6 and write up your Mindset Manual (pilot version), then get the Headspace app on a free trial. This will give you plenty to get you going. If you don't have your notebook, just use a few sheets of paper. Done is better than perfect.

Identify somewhere you will read your manual and meditate without being disturbed the next day. Put your manual in that location the night before, so you are not searching for it in the morning. Test the Headspace app. Set your alarm for 15 minutes earlier in the morning, and try to get to bed early. Get ready for "5, 4, 3, 2, 1" up and out of bed (Chapter 15).

Day 1

When your alarm sounds, use "5, 4, 3, 2, 1" up and out. Get a glass of water. Now spend 5–6 minutes reading through your manual. Open the Headspace app and start with the first guided meditation in The Basics; this should take you 10 minutes. For the rest of the day, stay hydrated (Chapter 13).

Congratulate yourself – you are on the road to predictable success.

Day 2

Get up 20 minutes earlier than usual and follow the same procedure as day 1. Today, add in a little exercise: 1–5 minutes is enough. Just do jumping jacks or push-ups or select an exercise from Chapter 25.

That's two days down. Take the time to give thanks to yourself for a job well done.

(Send me a photo of you doing your exercise so I know that you've started)

Day 3

Follow the process for day 2 exactly.

Day 4

Follow the process for day 2. When you have completed your exercise, take a minute to review the last three days. Have you noticed anything different yet? Has your attitude to anything changed? Have you thought differently? If not, that's okay.

Day 5

Follow the process for day 2, and then, in the afternoon or evening, complete your Daily Planner (Chapter 11). Give yourself a treat for following through.

Day 6

Follow the process for day 5. During the day, review Chapter 10 on the Daily Check-In. Identify some candidates.

Day 7

Follow the process for day 6. Take some time to reflect on the last six days. Have you noticed anything different? Well done – you are now well on the way.

Day 8

Follow the process for day 6, but this morning spend a couple of minutes on the Daily Review (Chapter 9).

Day 9

Follow the process for day 8. Today or this evening, reach out to each potential accountability partner using the template in Chapter 23. Get plenty of sleep tonight. Do something nice for someone to celebrate your achievement.

Day 10

Follow the process for day 9. Ensure you are getting to bed early.

Day 11

Follow the same process as yesterday, but add in 5 minutes of visualization (Chapter 8). You may need to get up 5 minutes earlier.

Day 12

Follow the process for day 11. Today, during the day, eat for energy (Chapter 14), and then tonight set your bedtime so you get eight hours' sleep before getting up for your Daily 10 tomorrow.

You're there. It's done. You are on the way to forming a new habit. You deserve this. The game is changing. From tomorrow on, implement the Daily 10 each weekday and notice the difference.

A day in the life

Your day should look something like this when everything is up and running smoothly. Timing will differ to fit your schedule, family, and work commitments. This should be done Monday to Friday – take the weekends and holidays off.

6:30	Get up using "5, 4, 3, 2, 1"
6:35	Grab a glass of water and read your manual
6:45	Meditate using Headspace app
6:55	Visualize your vision
7:00	Review yesterday using the three "what" questions (Chapter 9)
7:05	Exercise for 10 minutes at least
7:15	Eat a healthy breakfast and plan for lunch
8:00	Check in with your accountability partner
9:00	[At your desk] Open your Daily Planner first, and follow your own instructions
9:00–18:00	Work through your Daily Planner, eat a healthy lunch, hydrate regularly
18:00	Complete your Daily Planner for the next day
20:30	Turn off screens, turn down lighting
22:30	Time for bed

My day looks like this, except that I spend 45–60 minutes on exercise, which means I get up earlier and go to bed earlier.

At first it may seem like a lot to get through. If you go at it full-on, the first week will require some commitment. But when you realize the benefits, it will become something you love doing.

The Game Changer Formula is a set of rules by which you can live your life. Most people see rules as restricting, but great rules set you free. They facilitate your goals and your freedom.

When my wife and I were on long passages at sea, we took three-hour watches. Our duty off-watch was to rest – to ensure our safety on the next watch. When we had our son, we continued the system. We had specific times in the night that each of us was on duty. That meant that if our son awoke in the night on one of Ursula's shifts, I didn't move. There was no debate about who would get up. I didn't feel bad that Ursula was getting up. I rested, and she did her shift. A few hours later it was my shift, and that was the rule. Rules like this set you free.

If you want to change your life, you need to make that commitment. Achieving a great life doesn't happen without it. It doesn't mean that you can't enjoy every minute of that life and every minute of that commitment.

The great news for you is that by working on your mindset and using your subconscious, you will become the person who just does this instinctively. It's like becoming a different person. You will have a bias for action and will automatically make decisions based on your plan. Sometimes you will stand back and say, "That's not me" or "I rarely do things like that." In the beginning, I thought I had become a new person. Later I realized that that person was already in me, just hidden behind all kinds of crap that I had picked up along my journey.

The Daily 10 creates a routine or ritual. Routine is the key to the achievements of most successful people. In his book *Daily Rituals*, Mason Currey describes a day in the life of 161 artists, scientists, and creators. If you look for a common denominator, like get enough sleep, don't drink wine, or delegate everything, you won't find it. But the answer is right there in the title: daily rituals. In their own particular way, everyone in the book has developed routines or rituals that they practise every day.

Implement the Daily 10 now.

If you want to change the way you live your life and reach your full potential, it is important you get started and feel the power of the Game Changer Formula as quickly as possible. If you put this off, there is a high chance you will never do it. If that happens, you will not achieve what you deserve out of life. You will get washed ashore wherever nature dictates.

To procrastinate on implementing the Daily 10 is a high-risk decision.

Start practising the Daily 10 tomorrow morning. Don't wait until Monday or the first of the month. Don't wait until you've had time to do your vision planning. If you are waiting for something to improve or change before you start, you're thinking on the wrong frequency. It's okay to get things wrong – think of it as practice. Every day you're practising.

Just do it now. You can follow up later with your vision planning (which you should definitely not leave out). You may find it a little challenging for the first few days, and that's okay. You may miss a step or two in the first week – that's fine too. Don't be hard on yourself. Congratulate yourself on the progress you have made, and be a little better the next day. Your biggest risk is not taking any risk.

*

In summary: If you want your life to change, you need to understand and commit to the Game Changer Formula, create your vision plan, and implement the ten steps of the Daily 10 from Monday to Friday. The first week may be challenging, but you will quickly realize that routine supports success, and you will never look back. If you fall down, just get back up. If you want to change and you've read this far, then live this for the next 12 days.

In the next chapter we will look at how this structure gives you freedom and empowers you to live a balanced life, which is one of the keys to happiness.

17. Balance

It may appear from reading this that I spend most of my time at work and live a very strict life. But that's not the case. I have a lot of other stuff going on. I have a busy family life, and I spend time with friends and extended family. I travel for fun and family; we have just returned from a month in South America.

> *People are about as happy as they make up their minds to be.* — Abraham Lincoln (apocryphal)

Free time is crucial to achieving predictable success. You need free time for perspective on all aspects of your life. You also need it for creativity. Downtime and time away from the office are very important to me and something that I prioritize. I try to get home at a reasonable hour to spend time with my wife and son. I get my son ready for school and walk there with him most mornings. We can chat and get his day set up for excitement and learning. I rarely work on weekends. We spend a lot of time together then.

Free time is crucial to achieving predictable success.

On Saturdays we swim. On Sundays I play rugby. I am fantastic at it, but that's mainly because I play against six- and seven-year-olds. It's a thing I set up called Kids versus Adults Rugby. It's as much to get adults moving as kids, and we all go for hot chocolate afterwards. On Tuesday evenings we are at Sea Scouts, where I am a scout leader. I do the cooking at home most other nights.

I couldn't do all this without the Game Changer Formula. It gives me the extra productivity I need to get everything done and still have time for my family. I set aside time for myself too, and I guard it stringently.

It may sound like I have a rigorously structured life that leaves little flexibility and free time, but it's the opposite. It is that structure that sets me free. You may recall my Power Vision, "Liberating ventures and family adventures". The "Liberating" bit is there for good reason. It's something that I fight for and that influences my decisions in choosing opportunities to pursue. We all need freedom to be happy.

A happy life means a balanced life, and the Game Changer Formula gives me that. Happiness is not a result but a state of mind. You can have it now if you implement the formula.

It's hard to be happy if you are always comparing yourself to others. Stop doing that. Compare yourself only to who you were yesterday. That was a key life lesson for me and one that I think about every day.

> Ship's Log: Nov. 29 – Position 19:03.170N 24:19.255W
>
> We had been expecting a tropical depression to affect us last night, but I think weather forecasting is 24 hours behind us. The severe winds we had the previous night, from the

depression and the 35 knots on Wednesday, is what was expected for Thursday.

At the end of the day we're out here anyway, and no forecast is going to change that; there's no running for shelter, although we could, with enough advance warning, put ourselves on the right side of a storm. The other thing that is odd is that no matter what way we turn, there are no obstacles, so without looking at any charts, we can alter course any way we want. Our navigation really is just to go in the right general direction and make the fastest course possible under the given wind situation. Even though we are cooped up in 42 foot of space, we have complete freedom. If we have an adequate supply of provisions and a lack of deadlines, we can go anywhere we want on the planet. Tonight I'm looking at the other planets and stars in the stellar surround and trying to grasp the space and time. Our little world shrinks again.

It's hard to be happy if you are working continuously for the next week or year. If you always think that things will be better in the future, you are not living in the present and it's impossible to reach happiness. Work towards your Power Vision, but live where you are today. Be present and satisfied with that.

One more thing that will help with happiness: Keep learning. I learn every day from myself, from other people, and from books. Learning keeps you happy by building self-confidence, creativity, and connections.

*

In summary: Freedom is an important part of being happy. You should not look at the Game Changer Formula as a set of rules to tie you down. It is the opposite. This is a structure that will set you free. Stop comparing yourself to others, learn every day, and live in the moment.

Don't expect everything to go according to plan from day one. In the next chapter we will examine some challenges you may need to overcome, and how to deal with them.

18. Calm Seas, Skilful Sailors

When you apply the Game Changer Formula, things won't always go smoothly. The process is easy for some people but not for everyone. From speaking with many people who are doing it, I have learned that some elements can cause a little difficulty. In this chapter you will learn methods for dealing with things that don't go according to plan.

> *Everybody has a plan until they get punched in the mouth.* — Mike Tyson

When we sailed across the Atlantic, the first time squalls chased us, we sailed right into storms. Sometimes we had to completely re-plot our course when the weather was particularly foul. None of this stopped us reaching our destination.

When we sailed back across the ocean, this time east to west, we had bigger problems. We left from St. Maarten, an island in the Caribbean. Our intended route was to bring us to Bermuda, about seven days' sail from St. Maarten, and on to Ireland. We never made it to Bermuda. Storms meant we ended up 2,000 nautical miles northwest, in the Azores.

That was an extra two weeks at sea without landfall. We didn't make it back to Ireland from there either. Instead, we made landfall in Lisbon. We were in the right time zone but the wrong country. Planning is important, but plans don't always work out. I still regard the trip as a success, because our main goal was to cross the Atlantic.

Ship's Log: May 14 – Position 32:51N 47:59W – Wind W Force 5, Heavy Swell, Rain, and Squalls

Altered course due south yesterday, away from our destination, in order to try and skirt under some nasty weather that is sending heavy swell down on us. The trailing edge of this system may well lie in our easterly path today, but we will hopefully have dodged the worst of the draft.

The swell is making life on board a little bit tougher. Sleep is more elusive, and the angle of the peeing arc in the toilet has altered substantially; there are many mistakes. *Cerys* is steering an S, like a drunk on a push bike. These depressions have presented themselves at much lower latitudes than expected. I am glad now of our decision not to make landfall in Bermuda – we could still be there.

I can't make out the wall of water behind us until the white fingers claw over the crest of it like tips holding onto a ledge. They reach from the blackness towards *Cerys*'s stern. She lifts at the last minute and they fail in their attempt to grasp us, passing underneath and destabilizing us for a while. The next one is not far behind but invisible yet. White water passes from bow to stern as we lurch. The oncoming wave flips the angle of the white water, velvet-like in its capacity to change tone and texture with a stroke. Then it's gone.

Your first 12 days are critical to your success with the Game Changer Formula. They are muscle-building days, which means they may be a little tougher. You will lay down the mind-muscle memory for the rest of your life. If you get 12 days done, your mindset will already have started to shift. You will probably have noticed some subtle changes. Your new mindset – plus energy, plus accountability – will place you in the best position in the current so you flow to your destination. Things will become easier and better each day after that.

In the beginning, things can go off track, and even throughout the entire process you will have hiccups. You should understand some of these things and how to deal with them.

>Calm seas don't make skilful sailors.

If there is a stumbling block, the number one rule is: Do not be hard on yourself. You've probably done enough of that already for a lifetime. It's okay. Just be better tomorrow.

Here are some challenges you may face. They are either challenges I faced myself or that I have helped people through. Some of them will look like roadblocks, but in reality they are just track adjustments that you take to get back on the plotted course.

Not getting started

At the start of this book, you made a commitment to yourself to change. Throughout your life, if you are like the rest of us, you will have made similar commitments, New Year's resolutions and new plans, many of which you have failed to implement over the long term. That's normal. As you learned in Chapter 2, you used your willpower to effect those changes, and it is not strong enough to do it on its own. It needs the help of your far more powerful subconscious mind.

Now you have an opportunity to change for the better – a window in time where the current can support you and carry you towards your dreams. In short, a game-changer moment. You must take the chance you have given yourself, right now. You need to get to bed early tonight, get up a little earlier in the morning, and get started. Now.

The longer you leave this, the less likely you are to implement it. You'll pick up this book again in three years, and you'll have squandered those years. Life is about execution, not planning. It's almost always better to do something, even if it's not quite the right thing, than to have done nothing at all. Done is better than perfect. Every time we went to sea, I was seasick on the first night. I went anyway. New things are sometimes messy.

Think about it this way. If you think you need more information, take action as part of your research. That is, if you're not sure yet that this is for you, and you want to do more reading, stop. Don't research anything further. Try this first, just the way you understand it so far. That's the fastest and surest way to know if it works. Don't read another line until you take the first step.

Procrastination

There's an island in the Atlantic about 500 nautical miles off the coast of Morocco. It's called Madeira, but I call it Procrastination Island. Here's why. *Cerys* was anchored in the small fishing village of Peniche on the Portuguese coast. We had been there for about ten days, and our next destination was Procrastination Island. Every morning for those ten days, we were supposed to leave. Yet every night we were still at anchor, because I was nervous about this seven-day trip with just my wife and me onboard.

I would think of all kinds of reasons we shouldn't do it alone, and every morning I found a great excuse to not go. I rewired the battery bank, refitted the domestic power, installed new halyards, waited for a weather window. I did everything but what I should have done. I never told my wife that I had this apprehension, because I didn't want to scare her. If she is reading this book, she's probably only finding out now. I was procrastinating, and I knew it.

I had a saboteur on board that lived in my mind, a doubter that told me I was not good enough for this. On the tenth day I called that saboteur out, I challenged him, and we talked it through in my mind. I changed my mindset, and we set sail that afternoon. That passage of over 800 nautical miles was one of the calmest on the entire trip. We made it in seven days — exhausted, but without difficulties. I had a new belief in myself. A new mindset.

Ship's Log: Nov. 7 – Position 35:46.250N 13:50.855W – Wind NE Force 1, Sea State Calm, Heading 218 T°

I should have said goodbye to Ursula as I slipped the stern line off the pontoon in Peniche at 12h24. I did not really see her for the next few days. This was our first long passage together and alone. I now understand what Johnny Deadly said to me many years ago in the Zetland Bar when he told me he "shared a double bed alone". We do 3-hour shifts and are groggy between, so apart from the necessary debriefing, we speak little and are for all the world like ships that pass in the night on a ship that passes in the night. We were of course nervous leaving, though neither of us spoke of it. Out of the harbour and pointing the sharp end towards a tiny island in the middle of a very big sea is quite daunting to us. What if we miss?

So calm now in the daytime and very hot. We have stopped three times to investigate sea turtles and a whale (unidentified). I guess we probably pass these creatures all the time, but in the mirror-like water you can see them from quite a distance. Now wind has picked up and *Cerys* is nicely tuned and generating an excess of power as we tow our water generator. We have good southerlies now and hope to hold onto them for the next few days. So we have passed the one-week mark and are still talking both to one another and to ourselves, although the latter seems to be taking a firm grip.

Here are some reasons you may procrastinate:

You're waiting for help.

Stop waiting. Do it now or take the risk of never achieving your goals.

The conditions aren't right.

They will never be perfect.

A setback proved it's not possible.

You will have setbacks. That's part of life. There are a thousand ways you can find for this not to work. You just need one way to prove it does.

You don't know where to begin.

Just take one step. Get your Mindset Manual set up, and you'll know where to go from there. Trust me, and review Chapter 6.

Nothing you do will make a difference.

The Game Changer Formula will put you in control of the ship, but only if you take responsibility. You have the power to determine who you become, no matter what has happened in your past. Everything you need is already inside you.

You are overwhelmed.

I get it. So are many of the people who try this at first. Take a couple of steps, and you will see a path unfold.

You're too smart for this.

Great – things should work out perfectly for you. You don't need this. Come back to it if you think there could be a better way than the one you've been trying.

You need to know more.

You have more than enough information to take action. Let action be your further learning on this topic. Once you have this up and running, absolutely learn more on every aspect.

Your schedule is too hectic to make this work.

There is a way. Find it, or you will always be a slave to your schedule. It's not a good way to live your life. The Game Changer Formula can free you from your hectic schedule. People are doing this every day who have small kids, are up at six AM, drive two hours to work, or work two jobs. You just need to make room for it. It comes down to priorities, not time. Doing this will make you more productive and will therefore create more time for other stuff.

You don't have the energy because you have so much else on.

Then you definitely need this. The Game Changer Formula will create energy for you. You just need to start. If you're completely burned out, start slowly and simply. Doing this will help ensure you're never burned out again.

This won't work.

Then you're right. Henry Ford said, "Whether you think you can, or you think you can't, you're right." This shows how much mindset determines your success or failure.

Fear of failure

Failure is simple: just take no action. Everyone fears failure. We looked at it in Chapter 1. Action can mean pushing towards what you normally avoid, moving into the discomfort zone, or doing what scares you. If you are looking for change, haven't been able to make sustainable change, and don't want to go outside your comfort zone, then that is most likely your biggest issue. To get what you want, you will need to push into the unknown.

No Power Vision

If you have run into a stumbling block because you feel you cannot proceed without getting your Power Vision done, don't worry. Yes, it is important in the medium term to ensure you are going in the right direction and will meet your targets. But in the short term, having the right mindset, energy, and accountability will get you moving in a pretty good direction and make it easier to adjust direction later.

Turning a wheel on a yacht won't steer it if the boat is not moving. You need water flowing across the rudder for steerage. The faster it's moving, the easier it is to steer. You must get moving before you can steer.

Not getting all the Daily 10 done

Some people struggle with one or two elements of the Daily 10. That's okay. Getting seven or eight out of ten is a great start. But do try to get all ten into your day to ensure success. If you are doing seven out of ten, concentrate on getting one more this week, another one the following week, and the last one the week after that.

Fatigue

Changes in sleeping pattern and exercise, if you're not used to them, can mean you get a little tired. This will only be temporary. Once your body settles into your new routine, you will find you have far more energy and can get more done than ever before. Ensure you are hydrating, fuelling properly, and getting exercise to help with your energy levels.

Practising meditation sometimes affects your sleep. As your mind becomes more aware of thoughts, it can sometimes keep you awake or even wake you up in the middle of the night. This is also temporary. It's like when sunlight shines into a room: you can see thousands of dust particles in the air. They were always there, but now they are visible and so you notice them like never before. When you begin meditation, it can expose thoughts you didn't notice before, disrupting your sleep as your mind works through them. Once you get used to meditation, that will dissipate and you will sleep better than ever.

Injury

Maybe you hurt yourself exercising and have to stop. With anything new that you do, start small and work your way up. Exercise is no exception. It needn't be hard work – start with what you are comfortable with, and increase by 10 per cent a week. If you get injured, find another, safe form of exercise until the injury has healed. If you are not used to exercise, please take it easy.

Travel

When travelling, it's difficult to keep a routine going. If you travel a lot, you must work it into your schedule. If you travel infrequently and arrive at your hotel at two AM with a meeting at eight, then you should prioritize sleep, without a doubt. In cases like this, use the emergency routine in Chapter 26. This is not a replacement for the Daily 10, but it will keep you on track and ensure you do not break your new habit.

Not getting out of bed

If you find it hard to get out of bed, that's okay. If you repeatedly hit the snooze button, that's a habit you should really try to stop. At the very least, set your alarm 15 minutes earlier. Snoozing can be bad for your mindset. When you hit the snooze button, you start to think about why you should be up, and the amount of stuff you need to do, and it puts you in a negative frame of mind before you even lift your head.

I used to use the snooze button all the time until I tried the "5, 4, 3, 2, 1" technique, and I have never used it since. Not once. I thought I would forget to do it the first morning, but it came straight to me. You could also try putting the alarm on the other side of the room. Do whatever it takes to get started, because it will soon become habit. Ensure you are getting your Early 8.

Not being able to visualize

Some people find it difficult to visualize images. We can all do it to some extent, but for some it takes practice. Remember that it's not all about images. Emotions, sounds, tastes, and smells are also important in visualization. Here are some tips to improve your capacity. There is no right or wrong way to visualize, and every practice will bring benefits. Treat it as fun or an adventure – it's important to enjoy it. Keep your eyes closed, and relax. If you see nothing, that's fine. It will take a while – just accept that. Visualization involves flexing the right hemisphere of the brain. If you're not used to that, it may take a while. Practise by visualizing simple objects you are familiar with: something in your house, or a childhood toy.

Colleagues

Implementing the Game Changer Formula will change you on the inside but may change you a little on the outside too. If you have become more productive or less stressed, and get along better with colleagues, people may notice. You may also spot opportunities that align with your vision that nobody else will see. Be aware that people may notice something has changed and may act differently towards you at first. If it's working well, share it with your colleagues if you are comfortable with that.

Home life

Home life may also change. You may be more aware of your partner's needs, and more accommodating and willing to understand different points of view. Minor conflict may occur over simple things like waking your partner earlier in the morning, not watching the last half hour of TV, and possible jealousy or lack of understanding of what you are going through. Know that these things may occur, and accept the other person's point of view.

It is normally not advisable to try to get your partner to join you in the process unless they show a specific interest. If they are uninterested in it, that could be difficult for you. You will probably find in time that they become interested in how you have become a better partner. That's the time to discuss it.

Criticism

Criticism by the wrong person at the wrong time can take the wind out of your sails. But the worst critic you will face is yourself. When you make a mistake or do something embarrassing, what do you say to yourself? My pattern was to swear and speak to myself in a tone that I would never use with anyone else. I rarely even realized it was happening. You probably allow no one to abuse you as badly as you abuse yourself.

We all have an inner critic. It finds weaknesses and compares you to other people. Stop listening to it. You show people how to treat you by how you treat yourself. Stand tall and be kind to yourself. Speak to yourself as if you were speaking to a close friend. If you wish to take care of yourself properly, you need to respect yourself.

Non-optimal days

You will experience days when things don't go according to plan. Occasionally the Daily 10 won't work out because of an emergency or interruption. Don't beat yourself up about it. Don't beat anyone else up about it either. Just try to learn from it and do better the next day.

Most days for me are good, but some days don't go the way they should. One Tuesday I woke up at four in the morning and could not go back to sleep. I had a minor procedure done on my leg the same day, and it sapped my energy. I returned to work after the procedure, limping and feeling sorry for myself, and I found it hard to get any work done.

I came home late, annoyed because I didn't do everything I had planned for the day. I should have just said to myself that these things happen and I should not be too hard on myself. As a beginner, you might find yourself in a similar situation. My advice is the same: Don't be too hard on yourself. Practise, keep going, and you will surely get better.

Stress

This is such an important challenge that I will devote the next chapter to it.

*

In summary: The first 12 days of the Game Changer Formula are the most critical to ensure success. If you don't start right away, you take a great risk of failure. Start now.

As with anything in life, things don't always go according to plan. You may need to overcome such hurdles as procrastination, stress, fatigue, and travel. They may look like obstacles, but they are just hiccups, and they all have solutions. Having the right mindset will ensure you can overcome them. Don't be hard on yourself for things that don't go to plan.

19. Responding to Stress

The Game Changer Formula will enable you to turn an unsatisfactory life story into a remarkable one. Stress can bring that unsatisfactory story back, threatening your achievement of predictable success, so it is important to deal with it. Stress is prevalent in our lives today. I've devoted this chapter to the challenge, so that you can minimize stress in your life.

> *Stress is caused by being "here" but wanting to be "there".*
> —Eckhart Tolle

Acute stress is a physiological reaction that prepares your body to deal with threats. We know it as the fight-or-flight response. It is triggered by the release of a hormone that prepares you for action by speeding up your heart, increasing your blood pressure, tightening your muscles, and pumping adrenaline around your body. In prehistory it may have saved your life if you were faced with a sabre-toothed tiger.

Today those defence systems are triggered too often. This increases stress and can damage your health. Though we live in relative safety compared to our ancient ancestors, simple everyday things still trigger the stress response: an email from your boss, your phone battery dying, continuous notifications, being unable to find a parking space.

All these stimuli make your body prepare for fight or flight, poised to escape or defend yourself – but nothing happens. (This is another great reason to exercise: it allows your body to do what it just got ready to do.) It is difficult to remove everything that causes the stress reaction, but you can understand it and learn how to deal with it more effectively.

Stress is your emotional reaction to the thing, not the thing itself.

I see stress as the gap between what you want to happen now and what is actually happening. How do we deal with that? It boils down to patience. Stuff will happen that you won't have control over. When it does, acknowledge it – but never attach yourself to it emotionally. Do not let it drive your day, whether it's a bad cup of coffee, a slow queue, or someone annoying you. Stress is your emotional reaction to the thing, not the thing itself. There is a gap between the provocation and your reaction to it. You can learn to use that gap to acknowledge the issue and react with patience and calm.

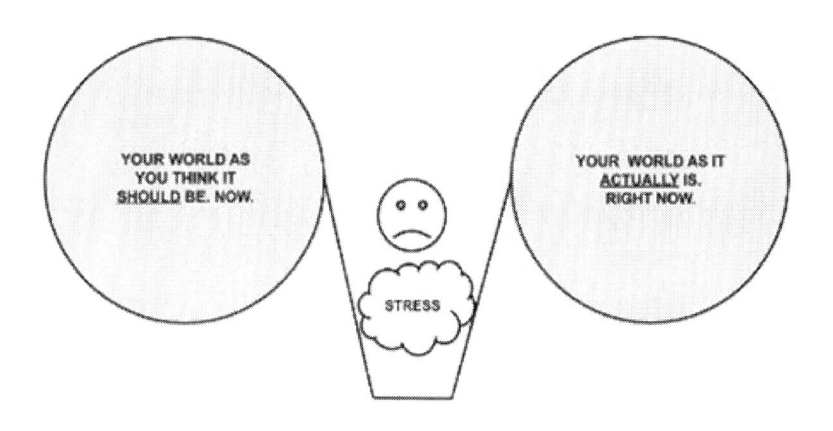

YOUR WORLD AS YOU THINK IT SHOULD BE. NOW.

YOUR WORLD AS IT ACTUALLY IS. RIGHT NOW.

STRESS

Patience is not about gritting your teeth and bearing it. It's about accepting the current reality. You can't change that. You need to acknowledge and embrace the facts as they are, but not allow them to affect you personally. Find and protect the calm that's already inside you, and don't let anything upset it. That does not mean you do nothing to remedy the situation. Seek to resolve it from a place of calm, patience, and ease.

When the *Cerys* crew reached land in December 2008, the first thing we did was a wobbly walk to the bar for a well-deserved steak and beer. After three weeks on a heaving platform, your legs don't cooperate on a solid surface. When we got to the bar, a stranger asked me earnestly if I was okay. I said I was great and expressed surprise at the question. He explained that he and some others had been watching me because I looked so stressed out. He was right: I was. But I didn't realize it was that obvious to a stranger.

At sea, much of that stress dissipated because there was no more preparation that could be done. Things often went wrong: We broke gear, got scared, and sometimes got a little short with one another. We were tired from being on shifts. We were sore from being thrown around the boat by the sea, night and day. You can get to feeling like everything is difficult and nothing is going right. It can get to you. But becoming annoyed or stressed can lead to poor decision-making, which is dangerous, so you must develop patience and not allow outside circumstances to dictate your frame of mind.

> Ship's Log: May 15 – Position 33:24N 45:22W – Wind NW, Swell 4–5 m

Bumpy night last night. Quartering waves on a confused sea pitching the stern up violently. My library fell on me as I slept, beginning with Isabel Allende and finishing – with a good thump – with *Reeds Almanac*. Luckily the concussing *Complete Sailing Manual* stayed put. In this weather using the toilet is a life-threatening rodeo, and donning socks, while necessary, is suicidal. I keep hitting my shins, and my swellings are now swollen.

Tried to use the toilet again and had visions of being flung out the door and across the saloon with my pants down. Honestly it probably would be accepted as quite normal to everyone on board. I managed to hang on, however. Clamping myself down with my hands stopped me from hovering in mid-air during this manoeuvre. I think I could manage quite well in zero gravity. The gravity of not being able to manage this on board would be far from zero, though.

Another way to find the calm within and remove yourself from the stress reaction is breathing. I learned this from the sea – this time from open-water swimming, not sailing. When I take my morning runs, I jump in the sea for a quick swim. Sometimes the weather on the west coast of Ireland is not ideal for a dip. In stormy or exceedingly cold situations, my swims can be testing.

One thing I practise when swimming in rough weather is finding calm even when the sea is raging. Go to take a breath on the right, and I get slapped by a wall of water. If I react without the gap between provocation and reaction, I will be in trouble, so I practise remaining super-calm and gently turn to breathe on the left. It's a fantastic drill that I take to work with me. When work appears stressful, I try to stay relaxed and calm at all times. It usually works.

When you're in a pressurized situation, a simple mantra can get you through: a few words you can recite to yourself. When I swim in rough waters, I use a mantra I learned from my son. He counts his arm-to-breath strokes: Bubble arm, bubble arm, breath arm. It slows things down for me and ensures I stay relaxed. I use it in all kinds of potentially stressful situations, even out of the water.

Remember that bad Tuesday I had recently? Here is what happened afterwards.

The Wednesday that week went very well. I got my complete list done. It was a relaxed day, and I walked out of the office and got myself a small beer to celebrate the day. Thursday wasn't as good. Things changed during that day, impacting my to-do list. By the end of office hours, I was not able to finish my list. But instead of staying longer, I decided to go home and have dinner with my family.

Tuesday and Thursday may seem similar: neither day went as planned. But they were very different in the way I responded. On Thursday, I did not beat myself up. I saw the gap and took it. I stayed calm while doing quite a bit of work. We are all learning, every day, so go easy on yourself.

You probably have a lot of things on your mind – things you worry about and things that cause stress. We all worry too much and are anxious about too many things. Many of these things are outside our control, so it is of no benefit to keep them in your circle of concern. Other things are very unlikely to happen, so there is little use fretting about those either.

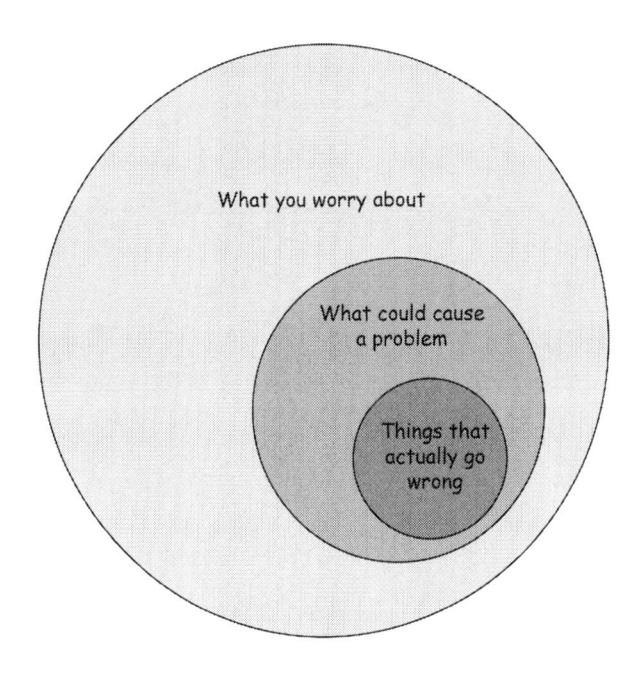

```
                 What you worry about

                    What could cause
                        a problem

                      Things that
                     actually go
                        wrong
```

If something concerns me, I ask myself three things. First, can I fix it? If not, I move on. Second, is it worth the effort to fix? If not, I forget about it. Third, what action do I need to take to fix it?

This means I rarely dwell on obstacles that are not fixable or not worth fixing. This annoys people sometimes, because they think I am ignoring issues. But it frees my mind to concentrate on what I should work on to move me closer to predictable success. Some of those issues will return another day, and when they do I review them again, because the situation may be different. And sometimes when you resolve one difficulty, a previously unfixable item becomes fixable.

Landed: On our voyage we have encountered seas of 5–6 metres and winds of Force 10. We have covered 2,850 miles and sailed for 501.5 hours. We have consumed 600 litres of water, 750 baby wipes, and we still have eight full auxiliary diesel tanks and 75% of our main tank. We have eaten two boxes of tomatoes, one of melons, two kilos of pasta, and a mountain of chocolate. We have read 19 books and 22 magazines (we have looked at the pictures in a further three). No razors have been used.

We have baked 25 loaves of bread, used two cylinders of gas, and ate all the cornflakes. Had no showers. We have eaten out of dog bowls while leashed to the vessel. We are now waiting for the measles to break out, and we cannot find the captain's auld dog.

It's a great feeling to be here, and as I walk up to check in with ARC, Customs, and then Immigration, I am very proud for us all. In Customs I am referred to as Captain, which makes a refreshing change from what the crew have been calling me. The island is moving, I want my money back, my kneecaps have two horizontal pains like eyebrows over the tops. That finished, it's 11 AM local time and a good time for a beer and a steak.

*

In summary: Stress is a prevalent issue that you will need to deal with effectively to achieve predictable success. Stress is your reaction to the stimulus, not the stimulus itself. There is a gap between what provokes the stress and how you react to it. You can learn to use that gap to react with calm and patience. This gives you control over your response. Reducing stress gives you greater capacity to achieve the life you deserve.

In the next chapter, the last in this section, I will show you some changes that the Game Changer Formula will bring to you and share some stories from others who have implemented it.

20. What Change Looks Like

Understanding what's in this book does not equal change. This book is not about motivation – it's about change led by positive action. In this chapter you will see how implementing this process has changed my life and the lives of others.

> *Your life does not get better by chance. It gets better by change.*
> —Jim Rohn

It doesn't really matter what has happened in your past, the times you have messed up, the failures or the rejections. At this point, all those things are just feedback, things that didn't work out that you can learn from. Nothing more. They are not who you are, but if you don't disconnect from them, they may determine who you will be.

All that matters now is now. The past is not living somewhere. It no longer exists. If you have implemented what's in this book, you are now disconnecting from the limitations of the past and opening yourself up to a bright new future that is limitless. It's like sailing across an ocean: if you don't risk it, you'll be safer for sure, but you'll never get to see the other side.

Motivational books and talks can help for a little while, but that inspiration wanes – sometimes within a day. The Game Changer

Formula and Daily 10 are things you will use every day for the rest of your life.

It's like crossing an ocean: if you don't risk it, you'll be safer for sure, but you'll never get to see the other side.

Once you have implemented this, you will lead a better life. You will be more successful in your work, your business, and your relationships, and you will be better at looking after yourself. You have a Power Vision. You'll find strength and commitment for it. If you work at it every day, with energy and a focused mindset, you will get there.

Here is what you will start to see.

You will find predictable success, however you define that – whether you want to make a difference in the world or live a life of significance in some other way.

You will find that things come easily to you. It's like freewheeling downhill. You will start to feel the flow.

You will experience stronger relationships with your spouse or partner, your children, and other people.

If you have a business, you will see more opportunities for growth, and you will experience less stress and a better, more balanced quality of life.

Personally you will be healthier, live longer, sleep better, and enjoy more positive thoughts.

You will have clarity on what you want out of life. You will have better focus, making you more productive at work and generally.

You will be smarter at selecting what problems to solve, and you'll solve them faster.

You will have more time to yourself, and you will be happier with yourself. You'll find that you are easier on yourself. Your inner critic will fade, and your inner voice will be more supportive.

You will have more patience, and there will be less conflict in your life. You will worry less about who you should be and what you should do, and you will notice that you are calmer.

You will be taking responsibility for your own life.

Your days of underachieving will be over, and you will no longer compare yourself to others but to who you were yesterday. You will be growing, learning, and improving by 1 per cent each day.

You will notice small changes at first, then they will grow and cascade. This is flowing with the current.

It will feel like a new you, but it's not. This was always inside of you but was just blocked out by years of negative thoughts and behaviours. It is like a blue sky: always there, but the clouds obscure it much of the time (at least in Ireland).

Where you used to be inflexible and closed, now you are open to new ideas, possibilities, and opportunities.

Where you used to have automatic negative thoughts on certain subjects, people, or ideas, now you are understanding of other views, and your thoughts are mostly positive.

Where before you had occasional success, some happiness, and a few spots of luck here and there, now you have consistent opportunities. You concentrate on empowering thoughts and ignore the disempowering ones. You make your own luck.

You now begin each day with intent rather than taking it as it comes. Your work is fun most of the time, and people want to join in.

You have complete clarity on what you stand for and where you are going. You achieve the levels you deserve in work, in relationships, and in your personal life.

You embrace change and thrive on it. Stress is gone, and you openly embrace the unknown.

Even your holidays are better. You commit to them, so that when you are off, you are really off.

You have a new level of confidence from the manual and visualization, and you are persistent. You are focused on work when at work, and on home when at home.

I know this because it has worked for me. I know this because it has worked for many of my friends, my team, my partners, and others who have come across my training. I know what I've worked really hard for over the last ten years. I feel like I've managed to get things done that others would consider impossible.

I was once asked to help a family friend who had been arrested in Thailand and was imprisoned in the Bangkok Hilton (a fictitious name for the Bang Kwang Prison). The prison is known for being overcrowded and disease-ridden. There is little clean food or water. He was sleeping on the floor in a cell, unable to lie down without part of his body resting on someone else's. Not like other Hiltons you may be familiar with. Thai prisons have some distinct challenges, and this one is known as one of the strictest in the country. His family had lost all contact with him and were understandably distressed.

I had passed through Bangkok once for two nights a few years earlier. That was the extent of my qualification for the search and rescue mission. I was unqualified when I took on the first Atlantic crossing, but this was a completely new level of unfit for purpose. But I was all they had, and strangely I was unperturbed by the mission. I was confident that I could pull it off, but I had no idea how. I just knew the next two steps: I bought a plane ticket and called everyone in my address book to see if they had a contact in Bangkok.

Ten days later I had tracked him down, coordinated his release, and was on my way home. He wasn't with me, because his passport was still at the police station. We had a scheme to get him out of the country without a passport. It was workable but high-risk, so I left him there for a while. He was safe and in contact with his family again.

On the return flight, someone asked me what I did in Bangkok. I hadn't had a moment to think about it until then. I found it difficult to remember all that had happened in those 240 hours. They were action-packed. I dealt with some fascinating people, some dangerous people, some influential people, and some wonderful people. It's a story that would take another book. But without the Game Changer Formula, I would never have had the belief or assertiveness to carry out the rescue. Things could have been very different for him if I didn't.

What follows are some other people's experiences with the Game Changer Formula – two short interviews, followed by selected quotes. Their reports are less dangerous than my experience in Bangkok, but they're all hugely significant in their own way.

*

I recently asked Dara how his daily routine has changed things for him.

What made you want to do this?

Well, I already had some morning routine, because I was doing t'ai chi and I saw the impact it could have, and I knew I was someone who could have done with more structure. So I decided to give it a shot.

What has been the main benefit of the Formula for you?

Discipline to stop the day running away from me, and it has allowed me to see the wood for the trees.

How long did it take you to get up and running?

I started in late October and kept adding bits on, and at the beginning of January I had my current routine in place. I do that now every day.

What do you do first thing in the morning?

I do some meditation, visualization, and affirmations first, then I do my t'ai chi and work on my posture for the exercise part. It takes me about an hour to do in total.

How do you manage to fit in an extra hour in the morning?

I changed the way we work at home in the morning, so now I take the kids to school and get up a half hour earlier, and that works for me. I get up at six forty-five now. I used to get up at seven fifteen.

How were your days before you started this?

Work was chaotic. I certainly would have let things slip, sometimes by accident, sometimes deliberately. I would sometimes get frustrated with the day. I didn't really recognize my achievements. Long-term strategy had slipped, and I was working from day to day. I was not at all satisfied.

What changed for you personally after you started?

I feel I'm in a steady state now, and I get less overwhelmed. Yesterday, in the car, one of the kids said to me, "I don't like Mondays." I responded by explaining that it was really just a matter of mindset. I now smile at the day. I'm smiling in the car, and I see all the other drivers looking unhappy. I get more stuff done in the day. I sometimes do the routine on the weekend too, and when I do, the weekend works way better. I find I am self-assessing quite a bit, and it certainly keeps me positive. It is so easy to do the opposite. It allows me to learn more about myself and about relationships. I am more grounded.

What changed for you at work?

Structure, mainly. I plan the day in the morning now and identify three priorities. I keep them in my diary and on my phone. Because I am better structured, it also flows through to my team. For example, we now have weekly meetings on a Monday and a ten AM meeting each day, which sets up the day for each individual and for the group. I ask them how last week went and what would make a great week for them this week. This creates structure in the office, and the team likes it. We are dropping less stuff, planning better, and things get done when they are needed.

It's also enabled me to step back and take perspective on strategy. I am more objective, and when the shit hits the fan, I see it but I'm no longer caught up in it. I am more attentive to staff.

In general, this is a great self-improvement tool. I'm not into self-help books and gurus, but this is certainly a game changer. I find I am sharing it with lots of people. I know it will help them. I enjoy it.

*

I also interviewed William.

What made you want to do this?

I was looking for a formula that worked for other people. I could see that this looked like it was working really well for you, so I thought, What have I got to lose? *I liked the structure of ten things to do. Other coaches have a bit of this and a bit of the other. You have it all and the subconscious and a process. Each part of the Game Changer process seemed to make sense.*

How long did it take you to get up and running?

I'm still not doing it 100%. I do a Daily Review, in that I look back over my to-do list for the day and make some notes, but not in a holistic and learning way like you suggest. I want to get to that. Also, my affirmations are all bundled together on the same page – I'd like to tidy that up. But it's taken me about three weeks to get to this point.

What do you do first thing in the morning?

I exercise first. I have an indoor bike, so I do spinning classes on YouTube for 25 or 30 minutes, although sometimes I change that for jumping jacks and push-ups. Then I take a shower, and I do my meditation after that. That takes five minutes. I then do my visualization. That takes about five minutes also; they can sometimes run over. I leave ten minutes for the Mindset Manual, which I read downstairs before leaving for work. I have started reading that in the evening too. I find that helpful. My affirmations centre purely around business for now. I also read my five key objectives for the quarter.

What do you do during the day?

I eat very well now. For breakfast I have berries, fruit, nuts, and seeds. I have written in my Daily Planner to drink three litres of water per day. I don't actually measure, but I have a pint glass that I keep filling up, and I am well over the three litres. I bring a healthy lunch to work from home each day.

Then, during the day, I work down through my Daily Planner and ensure I concentrate on my three priorities. Then I draw up my plan for the next day. I do that during the work day, just throwing a jumble of stuff in for tomorrow as the day goes on, and then I sort it out properly in the evening. On a Sunday I line out my main stuff for the week.

How do you manage to fit in an extra 50 minutes in the morning?

I get out of bed earlier. I was happy with seven hours' sleep, but now I get to be earlier and get up at six or go to work a little later.

Did you run into challenges, and how did you solve them?

The main challenge was to find a quiet spot in the house for visualization and meditation. I realized that hopping back into bed after exercising and a shower was the perfect place to meditate and visualize, so that solved the problem. Eating is okay – I'm relatively strict when I've set my mind to it, and bringing food [to work] helps. I do have a challenge in doing the Daily Planner – life gets busy. I should do it at lunchtime. My affirmations are too long; I need to refine a few sentences.

How were your days before you started this?

Pretty good. Exercise I thought was the key before I started to follow your guide of the Daily 10. Being able to influence the subconscious has given me an additional edge. I found with this you improve 10 to 15 per cent in one go, then the 1 per cent per day. First thing, I feel I don't want to do it, but five minutes later I'm more tuned in and willing to do stuff.

What changed for you personally after you started?

I have all but totally focused on work and career – my affirmations are purely around work. I plan on building in home and relationships.

What changed for you at work?

More focused on specific goals. On a commercial basis, I am more tuned in to my team, and I have clarity of communications. Quarterly execution of objectives is more focused on priority. I'm down to the 20 per cent of effort that is giving me a higher return.

What else could you say about this?

It is not a quick fix. It is an approach to life that will yield small but incremental improvements that over time will give monumental gains in the areas of life you apply it to. Not like a diet, it is sustainable.

*

Here are some quotes from others who have tried the process:

I now know that I am on the correct path with my life, and I have a plan to make it happen. I have the confidence to go out and just do things, as I know that with a few modifications they will work perfectly. —Rick, Melbourne

I am starting to feel more confident about myself and stepping out of my comfort zone to talk about our business to those around me. —Amber, Indiana

I remind myself daily of my life goals and achievements. And now I see evidence of a shift in my direction towards those goals. —Bob, Canada

My manual/journal has helped to keep me focused on my goal. —Vicky, St. Louis, Missouri

From the idea of opening a kind of digital marketing business in my hometown in Brazil, that led me to own a successful pub in my city. Successful

enough to make my dream come true. I'm very proud of the business I have, and I would like to thank you in person because you were the one that gave me an opportunity, and it was the everything I needed at that time to give an insight and how that escalated to what I have now. —Manoel, Brazil

It has enabled me to do more with my day, as I know someone will follow up. It helped me greatly keeping focus on my goals and not getting distracted. —William, Ireland

Your book has re-centred me and given me the reset I've needed, and I'm only up to Chapter 10. —Andrew, New Zealand

I had to take a good look at why and how I do things, both in my business and personal life. Work-and-play balancing act = happiness! Hard to do, but so worth it if we can accomplish it. With Rory's mentorship programme, this goal is achievable. This was a great process. Thank you, Rory. —Chuck, New York

The morning routine has definitely helped me in terms of being more focused and ready to start my day with a clear plan of action. Introducing meditation and visualization to my life has also helped to reinforce my positive mindset . Thanks, Rory! —Joan

Thank you for bringing tactics for getting past life challenges into this sales organization. Your personal applications have made it real. —Barbara, Georgia

Thank you, Rory, for spearheading this project. Your openness and honesty have shown me that mental focus and clarity are possible and I can remove some "old, deep-rooted baggage" that bogs me down and prevents me from being the best version of myself. Reading my manual every day gets me on

track and keeps me there. At this point I have many pages to read, but I can get through it quickly and find it sets the "tone" and allows my subconscious mind to flourish and rule. —Claudia, Canada

Since earlier this year, I've changed how I eat – I cut out all processed food, mostly eat very low carb, and avoid anything with sugar or artificial sweeteners. Energy levels have increased, and I've dropped almost 2 stone so far too. —John, Ireland

Remember: everything you need is already inside you. As Carl Jung wrote, "Who looks outside, dreams; who looks inside, awakes."

Part 4: Resources

All resources are available online at: RoryPrendergast.com/bookresources

21. Power Vision Process

Introduction

Do you know where you want to go? Not knowing exactly is a sure way to not get there. In Chapter 5 we discussed the Power Vision and how it can guide you to predictable success. To live the life you deserve, first you need to have a clear vision of what that looks like – and who you need to become to achieve it. Recall that each element in the Game Changer Formula is "to the power of" Vision. Developing your Power Vision is one of the most significant things you will ever do.

You probably have an idea of what you want but don't know how to get it. You need a Power Vision, and it must come from within. It will inspire you to achieve the life you deserve. There are many aspects to the Power Vision, one of which involves creating a plan. Developing your Power Vision will require diligence, but it will be time well spent. Your Power Vision is the direction in which you will travel for the rest of your life. It is therefore important that the course is right. Mindset, energy, and accountability will all be focused on this Power Vision, which in turn will amplify the effort you put in each day.

The plan you create will take the guesswork out of decisions and enable you, for the first time, to take deep and meaningful control of your life. It will give you a compass to show you where you're going, instead of a clock showing you how you spend your time.

To make it easier to work on, there is a downloadable version of the Power Vision Workbook here www.roryprendergast.com/bookresources.

The Process

Chapter 5 provided an overview of the Power Vision process:

1. Discover what you want

2. Create your Power Vision

3. Determine your roles

4. Develop your plan

5. Implement through the Daily 10

This process is about developing clarity about yourself, what's important to you, and how you are going to achieve it. You will identify what you want and what roles you need to play to achieve that. You will finish with a plan that fits neatly into the Daily 10.

When contemplating the questions in this workbook, you play the role of private investigator. The premise is that most of the answers already exist within you, and you are going to uncover them. Some of what you will need is hidden to you, so I encourage you to follow the process as best you can. Some questions or activities may seem odd, but they are designed to help you discover what you can't see right now.

Try to answer all the questions, but don't get bogged down. Enjoy it and I would love you to share your vision with me when you're done.

1. Life Now

Life Line

Draw a graph of your life up until now, marking the main events, people, and experiences that have shaped who you are today.

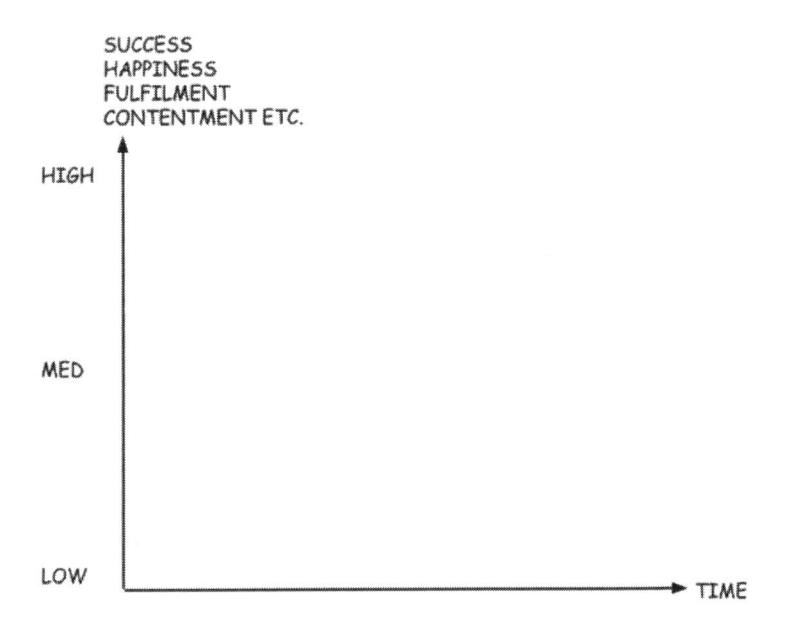

```
         SUCCESS
         HAPPINESS
         FULFILMENT
         CONTENTMENT ETC.
         ↑
  HIGH   │
         │
         │
         │
  MED    │
         │
         │
         │
  LOW    │
         └─────────────────────→ TIME
```

List at least five things you are passionate about.

1

2

3

4

5

List 10 of your favourite things to do.

1

2

3

4

5

6

7

8

9

10

What are your accomplishments? List these chronologically, starting with your childhood achievements. They do not have to be huge events; anything you're proud of is an accomplishment.

Complete a Power Vision SWOT analysis on yourself. Strengths and Weaknesses are internal. A strength could be confidence or tenacity. A weakness could be aggression or impatience. Opportunities and Threats are external. An opportunity could be to make better use of your communication skills. A threat could be your aggressive behaviour damaging your close relationships.

Strengths Qualities you displayed in your greatest achievements:	Weaknesses Weaknesses or deficiencies in your behaviour or attitude when you experienced failure:
Strengths others would say you have:	What triggers you to become negative? What are you most afraid of?
Opportunities	Threats

What is your number one strength or superpower?

Write a 30-second presentation about YOU. This will help you tune in to who you are. Imagine you are going to present your best self. How would you articulate your best qualities and talents? Have fun! Draw if you wish.

My name is …

My core strength or superpower is …

The things people like about me are …

I'm most passionate about …

The reason I care about this is …

The one impact or change I want to make most in the world is …

Three things I love doing most are …

I'm a good friend because …

I'm a good family person because …

I believe I have the following qualities …

I believe I'm talented at …

2. Life in the Future

Clarify your priorities by finishing the following statements:

My best talent is ...

The most important things in the world to me are ...

Values: Give shape and definition to your character. Think of a favourite hero, someone you really admire or who inspires you. They may be real or fictional, from the past or present. What qualities do they possess that appeal to you?

My Hero	Qualities

Recall a time in your life when you felt proud of yourself and made a stand on an important issue. Maybe you stood up for something that you felt was right, despite a lot of opposition.

What values were you protecting? List one or two. It's best to think these through yourself, but here are some ideas if you're stuck:

Ambition, competency, equality, integrity, service, responsibility, respect, dedication, diversity, improvement, enjoyment/fun, loyalty, credibility, honesty, teamwork, excellence, accountability, efficiency, dignity, collaboration, empathy, accomplishment, courage, wisdom, independence, security, challenge, influence, learning, compassion, discipline/order, generosity, persistence, optimism, dependability, flexibility, peace, success, truth, family, wealth, authenticity, happiness, justice, love, friendship.

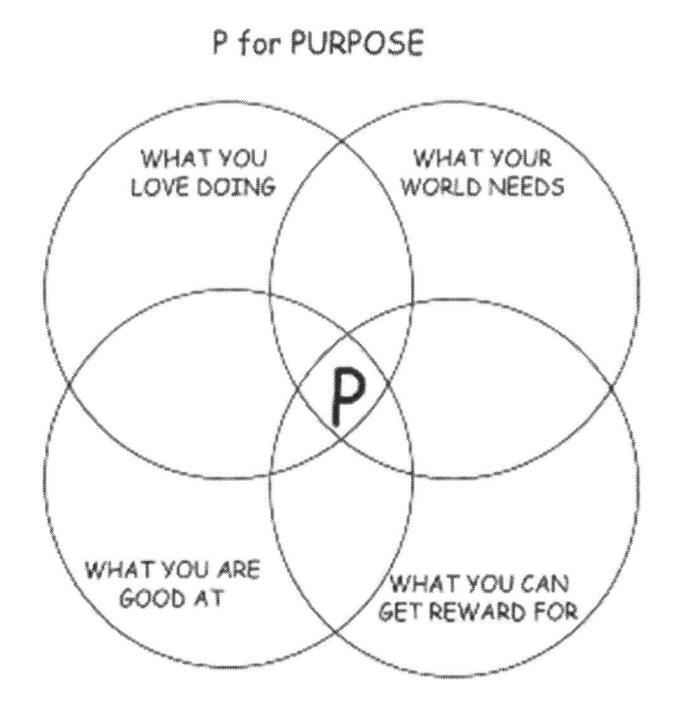

P for PURPOSE

What You Love Doing is your *Passion*

What do you love doing? What do you love to experience, that you would miss if you were unable to do it? What is your passion? What would you pay to do? What would you do if you had unlimited resources?

What Your World Needs is your *Impact*

What does your world need? What frustrates you that you really want to improve or change? What impact would you like to have? You define "your world" – it can be personal, family, business, community, national, or global.

What You Are Good At is your *Talent*

What are you good at? What are your gifts? What is your talent? One rule: modesty is banned. Think about things that come easily to you, the kind of things that your friends ask you to help them with.

What You Can Get Reward For

You will most likely need to determine a purpose that enables you to earn. An alternative is to have a job that fits your purpose and pays for you to spend free time. What can you do that people will pay for? Don't worry about how many people or how much they would pay.

To help you discover your purpose, look back at your Life Line and note the main threads, motivating themes, or preoccupations. Compare these to your passions and favourite things to do.

Review your Power Vision SWOT and your presentation.

How would you describe this chapter of your life right now?

What is the title of the next chapter in your life?

Reflect on your work to date, including your values.

My True Purpose in life is …

> To use my [Passion] .... and [Talent] ....
> to [Impact] .... by ....
> ....

What will feel different when you are serving your purpose?

I will know I am truly serving my purpose when …

4. Develop a Power Vision

Experts on leadership and personal development emphasize how vital it is for you to craft a personal vision for your life. Warren Bennis, Stephen Covey, Peter Senge, and others point out that a powerful vision can help you succeed far beyond where you'd be without one. That vision will propel you and inspire those around you to reach for their own dreams. I've learned in my own life that if you don't identify your own vision, others will plan and direct your life for you. We looked at this in Chapter 5.

Begin with the end. Imagine a conversation in the future – in five, ten, fifteen years' time – with a friend you haven't met in a long time. Tell them, in the present tense, all about who you are now. It is important to understand that you are talking about who you are, not what you have accomplished. You are envisioning the type of person you have become: your qualities, virtues, state of mind, health, interests, and involvements.

You have the power to greatly influence who you will be, and to determine what version of you will result from this. Your Power Vision should involve your purpose and reflect bigger aspirations for yourself. Bolder than anything you've been so far. List all your resources, not just the one or two you usually rely on, like possessions and knowledge community.

For example:

> I have unconditional love for my spouse and children. I am a great friend. I make a significant impact on the lives

of all the children I teach.

I am a talented business owner. I love my work by helping people. I make a substantial income to support the needs of myself and my family.

I am a successful businessperson. My innovative communications technology business is ready for sale. I am married with children.

You can in time distil this further. My own, for example, is: Liberating ventures and family adventures.

Start with rough notes, and don't limit yourself to words. Draw an image or logo that represents your vision. Ensure it is aligned with your purpose and values.

Here are some questions to consider. In each area:

What do you want to happen?

What do you need to learn?

How much money do you need for this?

What character traits do you want to develop?

What do you want to give back to the world?

What should you let go of?

What do you need to stop doing?

What do you need to forget?

Who are you at your best?

What's your 100th-birthday speech?

At the end of your life, what have been your three most important lessons?

Then return here to make your statement to your friend:

In ten years' time, I am …

Reflect on the good work you have completed in these steps. Live this every day, and you will have a great life.

5. Your Core Roles and Goals

Now you have a clear Power Vision that supports your purpose. To make your Power Vision a reality, you will identify up to six key roles that guide and govern your professional and personal life. First, complete the following exercise to establish the level of balance in your life.

The Wheel of Life

Each spoke represents an aspect of your life. On a scale of 1 to 10, with 1 near the centre and 10 at the outside, indicate your level of satisfaction with each. When you have marked all eight, join the dots together. A perfect circle indicates perfect balance, but this is very rare. Examine the shape to see how balanced or unbalanced your life is.

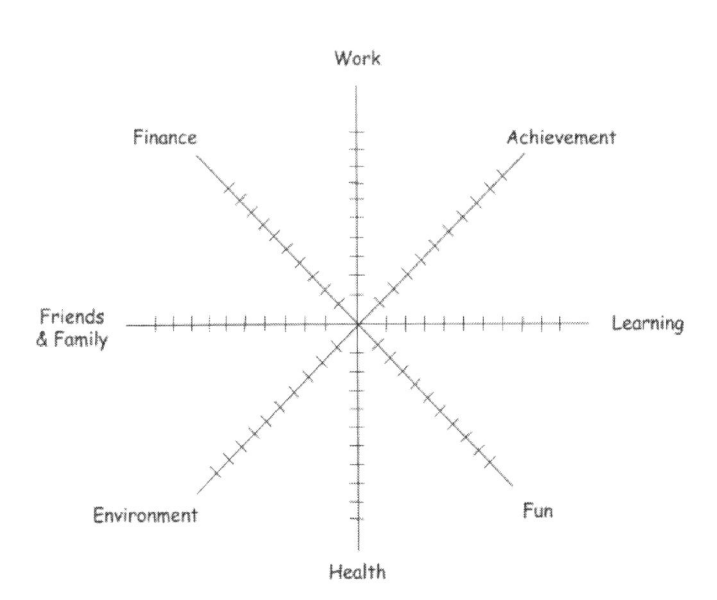

Use this exercise to determine the roles in your life that will require focus and effort to achieve your Power Vision while maintaining balance at the same time. These roles define your character and, along with the outcomes of steps 3 and 4 (Discover your purpose; Develop your Power Vision), help guide every decision you make. You will veer off course occasionally; accept this and make small but meaningful corrections to get back on track. Remember how this happened when we were crossing the ocean.

Think of roles in your life that are really important to you. Try to think about these yourself first. If you need help, here are some to consider: parent, friend, leader, family member, community member, neighbour, influencer, example setter, employee, son or daughter, sibling, business owner, investor, advisor, supporter, manager, youth leader, sport contributor.

Assign a small symbol to each role – something that will represent it for you, e.g. Health = ⎍⏦⎍.

The roles I will play in my life to support my purpose and achieve my Power Vision are …

Role	Symbol
1.	
2.	
3.	
4.	
5.	
6.	

No doubt you are not starting from scratch but have been making progress on these roles already. This is a good opportunity to acknowledge that progress.

Role	Symbol	I have made the following progress up to now …
1.		
2.		
3.		
4.		
5.		
6.		

6. Goals for Your Roles

For each of your roles, you can now establish something to aim for in the shorter term. Reflect on where you want to be with those roles in three or five years. Be visionary, creative, and optimistic. No part of your plan is written in stone, including your purpose and vision.

A goal should never be about stopping, getting rid of, or reducing something undesirable. Instead it should be about starting or increasing something desirable. Keep things positive, like we discussed in Chapter 6. For example, if you want to "reduce weight", convert it into something like "improve eating habits".

My three-year objectives for each of my roles are ...

Role	3-Year Goal
1.	
2.	
3.	
4.	
5.	
6.	

7. Inspire Yourself

The following exercises should help you to inspire yourself to achieve your goals.

The benefits of achieving each of my goals will be ...

3-Year Goal	Benefits for Me	Benefits for Others
1.		
2.		
3.		
4.		
5.		
6.		

8. Goal Strategies

Strategies are the leaps, the big how-to approaches that will help you achieve your goals. For example, to achieve my health goals, my strategies include exercising six days a week using different types of exercise, consulting with a dietician, and getting regular check-ups.

My strategies for each of my three-year goals are ...

Role (use your symbol here)	3-Year Goal (abbreviate it here)	Strategies: List 3 strategies (how-to's) to achieve your goal
1.		
2.		
3.		
4.		
5.		
6.		

9. Accountability Partners

The purpose of accountability partners is to ensure you stay on track every day and therefore achieve your Power Vision (see Chapter 10). You need to be humble enough to ask some people to help you on your journey.

Accountability accelerates your performance. When you are accountable to someone, the thought of embarrassing yourself by admitting you did not follow through ensures that you work towards your Power Vision every day.

People with an accountability partner are 80–95% more likely to achieve their goals, because what gets measured gets done – and what gets measured and reported on *always* gets done.

Checking in daily with your accountability partner also keeps you engaged in your activity. Just knowing that you need to report on it means you are more connected with your plan. Use the following format when you begin:

I will ask the following people to be my accountability partner. (See the Accountability Partner Scripts in Chapter 23.)

	Accepted
1.	Y /N
2.	Y / N
3.	Y / N

Do not skip this step even if you think you will be okay. Prioritize it. This is a key to success.

10. Action Planning

To achieve your Power Vision, you need a planning system: a simple, flexible process that breaks your path down into clear steps that you can work on each day.

To do this, you will need a trickle-down plan as discussed in Chapter 5. The key is to get from the long-term plan to the daily actions in simple steps. Here's how to do it. I call it the Vision to Daily Trickle-Down Plan. It is easy to create, simple to use, and very flexible.

You will develop a Power Vision Long-Term Plan that trickles down to a 12-month plan, which in turn trickles down to a quarterly plan and a "this month" plan, which trickles down to the Daily Planner on a weekly basis.

Each year, review the Power Vision Long-Term plan – one day

Each quarter, review the 12-month plan – one hour

Each month, review the quarterly plan – 30 minutes

Each week, review this month's plan – 10 minutes

Each day, in your Daily Planner, review this week's plan (your 10-out-of-10 week – Chapter 11) – 10 minutes.

VISION TO DAILY TRICKLE-DOWN PLAN

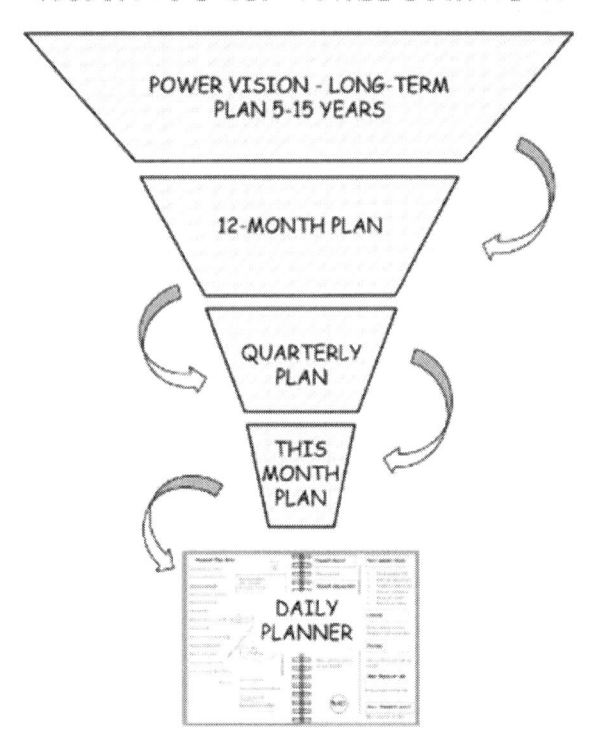

- POWER VISION - LONG-TERM PLAN 5-15 YEARS
- 12-MONTH PLAN
- QUARTERLY PLAN
- THIS MONTH PLAN
- DAILY PLANNER

You can get PDF versions of the plans and explanatory notes here www.roryprendergast.com/bookresources.

The templates overleaf may help you design your plans. These are the steps you will take:

1. Start with the Power Vision Long-Term Plan.
2. Add your Power Vision that you have discovered in the Power Vision Workbook.
3. Add your core roles – up to six, but it's okay if you have more.
4. Add your goals for each role and the dates and strategies.

5. You will update this each year.
6. Move on to the 12-month plan.
7. From your Long-Term Plan, fill in what you will work on in each role over the next 12 months only.
8. You will review this each quarter.
9. Now move to the quarterly plan. Determine what roles you will work on this quarter – I suggest no more than three or four.
10. Create a quarterly plan for each role, with details on the goal, why you are doing it, how to measure it, who is responsible, etc. Identify a reward for achieving the goal.
11. You will review this each month.
12. From your quarterly plan, identify what you will work on this month. What are your monthly actions? This will be updated each month and reviewed each week.
13. Daily Planner. Each week, create your 10-out-of-10 week. Draw down some action items from this month's plan, and add whatever else is important for you to complete this week (Chapter 11).
14. Create your Daily Plan each evening for the next day (Chapter 11).
15. You will now see that your Daily Plan is directly connected to your Power Vision. This is your daily traction. Along with the Daily 10, it is the power that will bring you predictable success.

POWER VISION LONG TERM PLAN [year X – year Y]

Review annually - one day

	1	2	3	4	5	6
MY POWER VISION IS:						
I WILL BE THIS PERSON:						
MY CORE ROLES ARE						
MY GOALS FOR THESE						
THE STRATEGIES I WILL USE ARE						
I WILL ACHIEVE THESE BY						

12 Month Plan [Month X to Month Y]

Include only three or four roles - review quarterly - one hour

Role	Goal 1	Goal 2	Goal 3	Goal 4

Quarterly Plan

Include only three or four roles - review monthly - thirty minutes

		Q1	Q2	Q3	Q4
Role					
What					
Why					
How					
Who					
When					
Measure					
Reward					

You will need one of these for each role

This Month's Plan

[My vision is]

To inform my 10:10 Week in my Daily Planner - review weekly on [Day] - ten minutes

This Month's Actions		
1	4	7
2	5	8
3	6	9

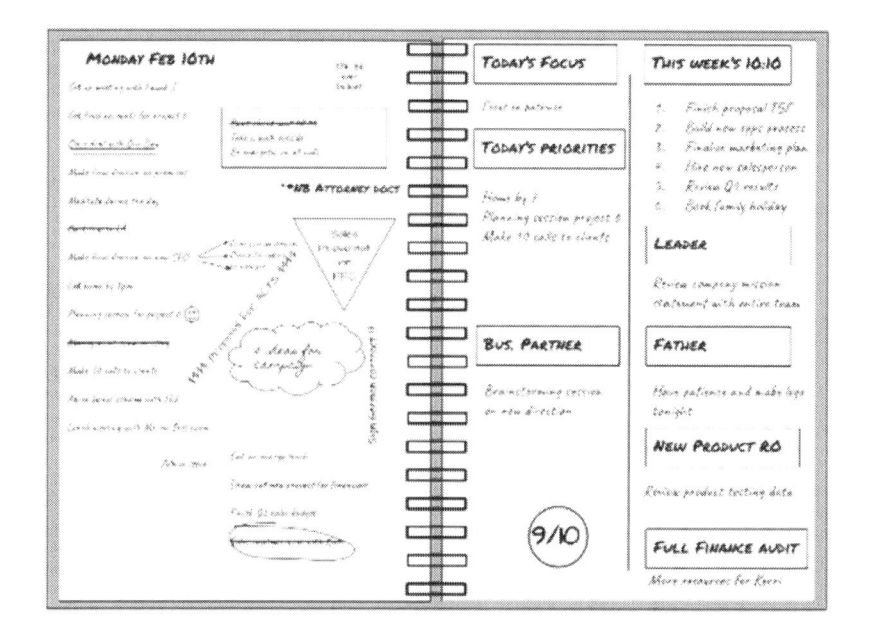

Action is the one step the universe puts in our way – otherwise everything would be just too easy. Action is the differentiator.

The planning process that I've detailed here, when combined with the rest of the Game Changer Formula, will ensure you take action every day that is directed at your Power Vision. The Power Vision is what you aim at. What you aim at determines what you see; the rest is hidden. You cannot aim at anything if you don't follow the formula.

22. Sample Mindset Manual

You can use this sample Mindset Manual to get started. A downloadable version is available here www.roryprendergast.com/bookresources.

Why is it that I love getting my Daily 10 done each day?

1. Read my Mindset Manual

2. Practise stillness for ten minutes

3. Use imagination for five minutes

4. Daily Review, five minutes

5. Movement

6. Write my Daily Planner for the next day

7. Fuel myself for energy

8. Hydrate for body and brain

9. Check in daily with my accountability partner [insert name]

10. Early 8 – bed early, up early, eight hours

Why is it that I love connecting to that feeling of getting impossible done

Why is it that I love knowing that I am more than good enough for all my roles in life?

Why is it that I love that I have all the ability I need to get everything done in the day?

Why is it that I love writing my full to-do list for my next day in advance, start to finish, which completely programs my subconscious mind and allows me to live my day in the flow and in the present?

Why is it that I love letting go of being hard on myself and only praising the young person that I am?

Why is it that I love prioritizing, and having fun doing the priority stuff?

Why is it that I love having all the time in the world for all my roles and taking ten deep breaths focusing on my role ahead?

Why is it that I love knowing that from this moment on, every thought I have is either a disempowering thought or an empowering thought – and I choose only the empowering ones?

Why is it that I love never comparing myself to anyone else, only to the person I was yesterday?

Why is it that I love knowing that my job is to make my eyes smile, and to make all my roles' shine by connecting with their passions?

Why is it that I love being a 10-out-of-10 communicator with my family and allowing myself to be vulnerable?

Why is it that I love knowing that all I need is within?

Why is it that I know that knowledge is power but is useless unless it's used every day?

Why is it that I love doing each task as an exciting adventure throughout the day?

Why is it that I love understanding my top developed values, and other people's values, and having the compassion to meet them at their values?

Why is it that I love living from my open, loving, and forgiving heart?

Why is it that I love being number one, being a champion at everything I do, and living the free life that I love?

Why is it that I love releasing myself from the old baggage, living now with happiness, adventure, and freedom?

Why is it that I love projecting my circle of happiness and everyone picks up on that energy?

Why is it that I love recognizing and playing with my inner child?

Why is it that I love identifying what's getting in the way of my natural state of joy, kindness, and empathy?

Why is it that I love being present throughout the day in the small actions?

Why is it that I love practising a random act of kindness each day?

Why is it that I love giving my family everything they need to be happy?

Why is that it I love connecting with my family in their world?

Why is it that I love integrating my new empathy and values with my extended family?

Why is it that I love clearly recognizing and continuously improving on all my roles?

    Role 1:
    Role 2:
    Role 3:

Why is it that I love being fit, fast, and flexible now?

Why is it that I love stretching throughout the day?

Why is it that I love having achieved my financial goal of [insert goal] in profit?

Why is it that I love knowing that I will always have more than enough money, because one of my businesses delivers [insert goal] a year?

Why is it that we love having already made [insert goal] plus, on [insert project], with zero hassle?

Why is it that I love improving my DDD each day – decide, delegate, disappear?

23. Accountability Partner Scripts

In Chapter 10 we looked at the Daily Check-In. We discussed accountability partners and how to find them. You will make a shortlist of potential partners and list their characteristics that could be advantageous or disadvantageous. Shortlist two people and chat with them by phone or over a coffee.

Here is a script for approaching them. You can email them initially and then follow up, ideally with a face-to-face meeting or at least a phone call.

Initial contact:

> Hi [insert name],
>
> I am working on something to help me achieve my goals, and I could do with independent input.
>
> I admire the way you … [manage to achieve your goals] [always talk straight] [always seem to be on top of things]. And I wanted to see if you would be open to having a conversation about helping me with accountability.
>
> If you are up for this, let's [meet for a coffee] [set up a call] later this week. If you feel this may not be a good fit for you, for any reason, just let me know. I would completely understand.
>
> [Sign off]

First meeting or call:

> Thanks for talking the time to talk.
>
> Here is what I'm trying to do. I've tried multiple times to set goals, and I've failed. I realize now that that's not unusual – it happens to a lot of people. I've learned that one way to overcome the problem is by having someone who checks in with me regularly to make sure I'm on track.
>
> I have a ten-step process that I want to run each day. I know that if I do that, I'll achieve [goal or vision] – but I need help to stay on track. Would you be open to helping me by being my accountability partner? We could try it out for a couple of weeks to see how it goes.

Now you can begin to explain the Game Changer Formula and, if appropriate, share the book with your new accountability partner.

Once you have agreed, it's time to set up the process with them. Here are some questions you will need to answer together:

- How will you communicate?

- How long is the trial, and how do you determine if it's working for both parties?

- When will you check in?

- What happens if you don't check in?

- What happens if the accountability partner doesn't follow up?

- What happens if you miss a day?

- How do you want your accountability partner to treat setbacks?

- What do you do when your accountability partner is on vacation?

- How do you keep things positive?

- How will you review the project with each other, and when?

- What can you do for your partner in return?

Discuss your goals and ensure the partner has a copy of them. Make a commitment to honesty on both sides. Remember, this is a commitment by your accountability partner also.

24. Sample Meditation

Here is a seven-step meditation practice written by Kadam Adam Starr, principal teacher at Tara Kadampa Meditation Centre, Dublin. I have attended a number of Adam's talks at our local university.

A seven-step practice:

The function of meditation is to help us to develop and maintain a calm, clear, and peaceful state of mind, at all times, in all situations. Firstly, we will discover what meditators have known for thousands of years. This experience of inner peace, or peace of mind, is a real source of genuine happiness and well-being. Secondly, this feeling of happiness, contentment, and well-being – that is the result of regular meditation practice – also helps us cope with the busyness and difficulties of daily life. So much of the stress and tension we normally experience comes from our mind, and many of the problems we experience, such as ill health, are caused or aggravated by this stress.

Just by doing a simple breathing meditation practice for ten to fifteen minutes each day, we will reduce this stress. We will experience a calm and spacious feeling in the mind, and many of our other problems, including anxiety, fear, and negative thinking, will begin to fall away. Finally, meditation also enables us to tune in to, and cultivate, our inner potential for good qualities, such as loving kindness, compassion, and wisdom. This helps us relate to ourselves, others, and the world around us in wiser and healthier ways, which significantly improves the quality of our life and relationships.

This is a simple, seven-step breathing meditation practice that anyone can enjoy:

1. Find a quiet place to sit (a chair is fine) that is free of distractions. Partially close your eyes. Back straight but relaxed. Hands resting in your lap. Breathe gently and naturally through the nostrils. Let go of focusing externally, and gather your awareness inwards.

2. Begin by generating a wish to use the meditation to improve your inner peace, happiness, and good qualities, so that it will be of benefit to both yourself and others.

3. Next, be aware – without judgement – where your mind is at, in this moment. Is it calm, clear, and peaceful? Or busy and distracted? To let go of agitation and distraction, and centre in a calm, clear, and peaceful state of mind. Focus – without distraction – on the sensation of breath as it enters and leaves through your nostrils.

4. When you notice you are following thoughts and distractions, simply acknowledge and accept their

presence, and let go of the urge to follow them. Then relax and return to the breath, allowing your attention to draw closer and closer to the breath each time.

5. Eventually your attention will rest on the breath, and you will notice the distractions naturally dissolve, like waves returning to an ocean. You will feel a deepening sense of inner calm, clarity, and peace of mind.

6. Just relax into this inner peace, and identify with it as your potential to change, to find a deeper and longer-lasting peace of mind and happiness. Thinking: If I can become a little more peaceful, a little happier through a little meditation, it follows that I can become a lot more peaceful, a lot happier, through regular meditation.

7. Conclude the meditation with a determination to maintain this inner calm and peace throughout your day, so that it naturally, and positively, influences everything you think, say, and do.

25. Exercise Routines

Here are some simple exercise routines, all of which you can do at home and most of which don't require any equipment. You'll find workouts for beginners, older adults, and active individuals. Choose one to get you started, but search YouTube for workouts that suit you.

10-minute six-pack workout with no equipment

www.youtube.com/watch?v=Q-vuR4PJh2c

10-minute core routine from Daniel at Fitness Blender

www.youtube.com/watch?v=h8qNmVJ_jI8

12-minute home yoga practice from Dave Cunningham of Yoga Shala (my yoga teacher)

www.youtube.com/watch?v=pM4vWKwXD84

20-minute intense cycling workout, if you have an indoor bike

www.youtube.com/watch?v=gGGvKt8vWho

10-minute cardio workout you can do anywhere

www.youtube.com/watch?v=gUWFmn8f3H4

5-minute push-up workout

www.youtube.com/watch?v=LWhENdAizkE

5-minute fast yoga break with Adriene

www.youtube.com/watch?v=nQFf38xeBww

10-minute indoor bike warm-up

www.youtube.com/watch?v=XVlXHG-P9YY

10-minute Pilates workout with Lottie

www.youtube.com/watch?v=qyeB2Wdh3cc

10-minute seated exercise for older adults

www.youtube.com/watch?v=6Ts-deSDnRM

10-minute low-intensity beginner workout

www.youtube.com/watch?v=g-D7ncAC9rQ

10-minute dance workout for beginners

www.youtube.com/watch?v=9_MxwQw10RI

7-minute running warm-up

www.youtube.com/watch?v=Kdgv6DPAZBU

5-minute running cool-down

www.youtube.com/watch?v=CWOq-PL396I

Pre- and post-run stretches

www.youtube.com/watch?v=qq1kGDd4Q60

10-minute jump rope workout

www.youtube.com/watch?v=1BZM2Vre5oc

6-minute guide to power walking

www.youtube.com/watch?v=55flVWE0wkA

10-minute home boxing exercise

www.youtube.com/watch?v=pWLEkO0MlXs

10-minute home stairs exercise with Holly

www.youtube.com/watch?v=Y1-uwSGuD5w

26. Emergency Morning Routine

In Chapter 18 we discussed things that can throw you off course. One of those is travel. If you travel regularly, then you need to build your routine into your travel so that it works seamlessly.

If you sometimes find yourself arriving at a hotel late after a long day travelling, and you have only a six-hour window of sleep before an early-morning meeting, then you can use the Emergency Morning Routine. It can also be used for other situations where you need to prioritize sleep, for example if the kids were sick during the night. It takes just four minutes.

1. As soon as you wake up, take out your Mindset Manual and read ten affirmations. Any ten. That will take you one minute.

2. Sit on the side of your bed and meditate with a breathing exercise for one minute. All you need to do is count your breaths. One for in, two for out, etc. When you reach ten, start from one again. As your mind wanders, bring it gently back to your breath. If you lose count, no problem: start from one again.

3. Stand up and do 15 seconds of jumping jacks, then 15 seconds of push-ups, even if you only manage a

couple. Run on the spot for 15 seconds, then stretch for 15 seconds. Any stretching that feels good. That's another minute.

4. Lastly, spend a minute visualizing the day. Determine what you want to get out of it and what feeling that will give you. Visualize that feeling.

Do these four things for four minutes, and I guarantee you will have a better and more successful day when travelling. Note, though, that the emergency routine should only be used every once in a while. If you find you are using it regularly, you need to look at your day and see how to fit things in better.

27. Recommended Books and Other Content

What follows are some of the best books and other content that I have read or consumed over the years and that can help you attain predictable success faster. In this book I have concentrated on giving you the minimum information you need to get results quickly and easily. Once you are up and running with the Game Changer Formula, you may wish to dive a little further into some of the elements or to add new ideas.

Links to all these books and resources are available at www.roryprendergast.com/bookresources

Making Money Is Killing Your Business by Chuck Blakeman

If you are a business owner or intend to become one, you simply must read this book. Chuck breaks down the reality of being a business owner and shows you how to build a business that can operate without you in three to five years. His ideas are simple, and every business owner should be operating from this book as if it was a manual.

Traction by Gino Wickman

A must-read if you have a business and operate with a team. Gino's book introduces a system for managing your business with ease. It fits in well with *Making Money Is Killing Your Business*. In *Traction* you will learn how to plan and how to run your business communications and numbers efficiently. It's like a Daily 10 for business.

Profit First by Mike Michalowicz

Mike shows you in this book how to turn your business into a money-making machine and how to put an end to cash-flow issues and lack of profit. This book is for business owners or managers.

Into the Magic Shop by James R. Doty MD

This is a neurosurgeon's journey through understanding how the mind works and how it can be changed or upgraded to achieve whatever you desire. It is not a technical or medical book – it's about the author's experiences as a child and how learning mind exercises changed his life. It will give you an excellent insight into the imagination and visualization.

Think Bigger by Michael Hill

In this book, Michael talks about what has made him successful in international business. Of particular interest is his idea of long-term planning and positive thinking. He shows how meditation has had a major impact on his life and discusses food and fun as important aspects of his success.

Get it here:

The Tibetan Book of Living and Dying by Sogyal Rinpoche

This is a book about how to live and how to die, but it has also taught me a lot about meditation. If you want to explore meditation further, then I highly recommend this book.

The Pressure Principle by Dr Dave Alfred MBE

Dave Alfred has coached some top sportspeople, who often end up in highly pressurized situations. His book explains how pressure works in sport and how to overcome it. There are huge learnings here for everyone on handling stress, dealing with pressure in everyday life, and maintaining composure in high-pressure situations. An excellent read, and not really a sports book.

The Three to Five Club

Not a book but a group of likeminded business owners who get together twice a month with a facilitator or trainer to cover a syllabus based on Chuck Blakeman's ideas from *Making Money Is Killing Your Business*. For many years I was a member of one of these mastermind groups, facilitated by John Heenan. Chuck has these groups all over the world, each run by a local facilitator trained by Chuck's Crankset team. You will learn how to build a business that operates without you in three to five years.

Find out about it here: www.3to5club.com

12 Rules for Life by Jordan Peterson

How should we live today? Jordan Peterson breaks it down to 12 rules we should adopt in order to live well. This is a fascinating read with interesting insights into how we think, work, and interact with each other. It will help you with confidence, direction, and relationships.

The Law of Vibration by Bob Proctor

Bob Proctor of the Proctor Gallagher Institute talks about how to tune in to positive vibration by changing your thoughts. This will lead you to operate on a frequency that will bring you where you need to go in life. You control your thoughts, therefore you control your destination.

See it here: www.youtube.com/watch?v=KawV9TbX85A

28. The Epic Project

You may have noticed some references in this book to the Epic Project, which is part of my personal Power Vision. I plan to live an enjoyable and active life to 120 years plus. I believe this is not difficult to do if you begin working at it early enough, have a strong enough vision, and implement the Game Changer Formula.

I currently believe there are four elements that need to be managed to achieve the Epic Project: body, mind, environment, and finance. Your body obviously needs to be looked after to reach such an age. This can be done with exercise, diet, and monitoring. For the mind, the two areas to concentrate on are mindset and brain function. The environment entails two things: being a contributor to your community (which can be defined in many ways), and to the planet itself. Finally, if you plan to live to 120 plus, then you will need to finance that. Most people don't even plan properly for 70 years.

This project is not something I have completely planned out yet. I have a lot to test, and a lot to learn, but I know I can do it. I plan to make it a project I will share with people, so that I can bring people with me on the journey.

Although I have started working on my own four elements, I have not yet put a system in place for sharing my learnings. That will happen in 2021. If you are interested in following that journey, and maybe even joining me, you can sign up here to be notified when it goes live: http://www.roryprendergast.com/epicproject

See you there.

Ready to apply what you've read here?

Every year Rory runs online workshops and events offering coaching on the Game Changer Formula and other areas of Predictable Success. He is also a guest speaker at conferences and events for business owners.

If you are truly determined to achieve predictable success for you, your family and your business visit www.roryprendergast.com or email team@roryprendergast.com now.

And...

If you liked this book please take the time to review it on Amazon.

Send a link or screenshot of a review or blog post you've written that features this book to team@roryprendergast.com and we will send you a thank-you and a complimentary invitation to an online event.

Thank you for reading The Game Changer Formula

Printed in Great Britain
by Amazon